URBAN SCHOOLS CLASH WITH 14TH AMENDMENT

The Politics of Race and Culture

Michquel S. McCullough

Madison Books Express

Madison

Canton

Table of Contents

Introduction 3

   1. Equal Protection Argument 13

   2. My Story 22

   3. Court Action 1 33

   4. A Constitutional Crisis 48

   5. Beyond Race, Segregation, Desegregation and Re-segregation 67

   6. Make America Great Again 75

   7. Education is Democracy 90

   8. From Urban School to Incarceration 101

   9. A Public Policy Crisis 117

   10. Time for Due Process 124

   11. Let Your Voices Be Heard 134

   12. Teachers Must Fill the Gaps 146

   13. One Black President, One Thousand Black Inmates . 162

   14. Black Churches on Every Corner 176

   15. Court Action Part II 189

Author's Note 219

ACKNOWLEDGMENTS 221

References 224

Introduction

In April of 2019, thirty-three rich and successful Hollywood elite were charged with conspiracy to aid and abet their kids in a college admission scam. The complaint alleged among things—money laundering, falsifying information to give their kids a competitive edge and cheating on college admission exams so they may attend some of the best colleges and universities in the country.[1] If I decided to say nothing else, this incident will further prove my point that I will press repeatedly. That is, urban students are at a supreme academic disadvantage, but not impossible to compete against students that attend private and suburban schools.

These parents unequivocally understand the value of education and the significance of a great post-secondary education. Within that same light, I am inclined to assume that these parents would have never allowed their kids to attend an urban school. I am inclined to assume that these parents also understand that one's ability to achieve life, liberty, and property as expressed by the 14th amendment is predicated on a good secondary education. My belief is substantiated by what prosecutors have alleged against them; thus, pleas of guilt by some. So, I ask you to not read this text in a vacuum.

I ask you to see urban students like any other student, and to determine that they deserve better than what urban schools are rendering.

Now that the stage is set, allow me to express what inspired me to write this book. First, I must thank my beautiful, loyal wife Mashenna, and my three boys Malachi, Martravious and Ojavien. They are the reason for my less radical and tempered existence. They inspire me daily to be great. It is because of them; I was able to write this book. Just to look in their faces rendered the continued strength, especially when doubt and fear attacked my thought process throughout this sobering journey.

My personal urban school experience demanded I avoided sending my boys to one. I thought about all the known factors and could never live with myself if I didn't give them the chance I didn't receive. I ask that you do not see it as derogatory criticism, but as constructive. The criticisms I will level are warranted, but more important, are to be viewed in a positive light. In order to solve a problem, a light must shine over it. This is the purpose of this book. I want readers to truly understand the urban student's situation. As well, I want you to realize what many of these urban schools are doing either through sheer ignorance, a complete indifference to urban student's future or because a disconnect between urban students and their current predicaments. Be assured I am aware of the funding gap between suburban and urban schools. This is a serious problem as well but at the core of urban school's problem is an inability to change its culture. A culture that must model a passion for knowledge, not just passing state mandated test. For some time, I have desired to write a book about urban school education. But I asked myself too many daunting questions, like, who will read a book that you write, or what makes you an expert in education, more important, what can you articulate that has not been said countless times. These questions fueled my fear but were superseded by a willingness and desire to paint a vivid portrayal to the world about the state of urban education. I like to think of these thoughts as a web of serious, and sometimes crippling emotions. Fast forward to 2017, while in law school, this idea rolled over me like rushing tide waters after taking a Race and Law class. My professor, Angela Kupenda, someone I consider to be a dear friend and mentor was a driving force behind the idea of this book. That class served as a litmus test for this book. She never permitted me to make excuses, and constantly reminded me that the process of law school was bigger than myself. I must admit she was right.

Race and the Law required a thirty to fifty-page paper. Without hesitation, immediately I chose urban education and its considerable plight as a topic. At first glance, I was sure I wanted to engage the topic "Practical Teaching as Leadership," but my professor induced me to think a little deeper, and more outside the box. To achieve this, she required that I write three two-page papers on a different urban education topic. After conducting significant research, it was evident that each educational stakeholder fiercely blames each other, and no one desires to share the blame. Through my research and the help of Professor Kupenda, my paper was entitled "Sharing the Blame, Hence, the Bounty, for Educational Transformation in Mississippi Urban Public Schools."

After engaging my topic in more depth, I found many individuals using *Brown v. Board of Education*, and its failed implementation as a basis for inadequate minority, poor, and struggling urban school districts. Engaging "Shared Blame" within the context of *Brown* sixty years later, was used to articulate the amount of time stakeholders invest discussing the problem, instead of working across the aisle to fix it. My goal was to yes, articulate what is true about failing urban school districts, and what some view as the *Brown* effect of inadequate education, but also to discuss the successes that did stem from *Brown*. Although there are success stories from urban school districts, there are not enough. This consequential fact prompted me to thoroughly and profoundly think about this issue.

As I sat at my desk one-night, free writing to explore the crippling effects and detrimental social conditions urban school students faced after graduation as I once did, I wondered why this an acceptable norm was. As I gauged the topic with agitated concern, the idea swooped in like an unanticipated tidal surge off the banks of the Mississippi Gulf Coast. Varying speeches delivered by Martin Luther King took over my thought process and uncontrollable tears ran wildly down my cheek bones. These speeches reminded me of Dr. King's dream and how certain members of this nation fought for black social justice and equality. While still mentally in another dimension, I thought about the true meaning of the 14th amendment.

"I got it," I thought, 'these schools are violating the 14th amendment."

I blurted!

"How though?"

On the surface, the question seemed simple to answer,

but I knew it required concentrated thought to understand the social constructs in place that aids urban schools to perpetually release urban students into society ill-prepared for what they undoubtedly would experience. I fervently believe that urban schools are not just clashing with the Fourteenth Amendment and a constitutional crisis exist. I also think that the black race and culture plays a part in urban schools' demise. This last idea suggests that we must think about our political and philosophy values as a country within the context of urban education. I wonder have we become a nation that only likes to speak in political abstractions because it's convenient and takes no practical work. Or are we a country that understands abstracts are no different than ideal? We can idealize much as we like about what true liberty should look like, but urban school students live in the real world, where certain education policies are hampering their chances to achieve this liberty we abstractly discuss.

If you ask me, many of these policies operate as a sham and our political and cultural new norms permits this sham to continue without consequences.

It would be misleading to suggest I am not fearful about urban student's future because of the current consequential damage urban schools have systematically committed. The ramifications are not some unfounded myth. This is real, and too many of these students are transitioning from classrooms to cell blocks, or from classrooms to government assistance payrolls.

We require states to provide a free public education, but at what cost. Are these so-called urban schools even worth taxpayer's dollars? Of course, I am being rhetorical, but think about the presumption. It is at least worth considering, even if moderately absurd. Within the constitution of each of the 50 states, there is language that mandates the creation of a public education system. The authority for public education falls to states. A 1973 Supreme Court case called *San Antonio Independent School District v. Rodriguez* perfectly highlights this.[1]

The law suit spearheaded by Mexican American parents on behalf of their children, argued that the Texas school financing system inadequately funded minority school systems because of the imbalance of property taxes received by affluent schools versus less-affluent schools.[2] The court held that the "consideration and initiation of fundamental reforms with respect to state taxation and education are matters reserved for the legislative processes of the various States, and we do no violence to the values of federalism and separation of powers by staying our hand."[3] Remember this key fact because it will be critical further alone as I imaginatively argue before the U.S. Supreme Court. The Justices punted the educational problem these parents believed to be a fundamental crisis. If they did not think so, why they would have gone through the burden of litigation to seek a better educational opportunity for their children. Inadequate funding is an issue, but it is not the driving issue. I won't resort to economic arguments because it will only muddy the practical problems needed to highlight the issues as I see them.

Lately, in the policy community, and on cable television news networks, you hear the term "constitutional crisis" mentioned quite frequently. But what does it mean? There are several different interpretations for the term of art. Linda Monk defines a constitutional crisis as, 'a breakdown of government functions that have a duty to resolve some issue.' Essentially, she conveys that when government fails to execute its proper duties in the process of carrying out processes and procedures to achieve some objective social policy goal, a constitutional crisis exists. I will push the needle by stating, when a government entity intentionally neglects its social objective obligations to the public or constituent group, a constitutional crisis may exist.

If this is the definition of a constitutional crisis, and each state has an objective responsibility to ensure public schools are educating all students, I would argue a constitutional crisis exist within the context of states and its urban schools. Although states cannot be directly blamed for urban schools' poor education system, it does have a responsibility to ensure urban schools are educating its students. Although, many state constitutions are clearly silent on what type of education a student should receive, this does not weaken my argument. In fact, my constitutional crisis contention helps strengthen and bolster my position that urban schools are clashing with the 14th amendment.

Mississippi Constitution of 1890, section [201], states that "The Legislature shall, by general law, provide for the establishment, maintenance, and support of free public schools upon such conditions and limitations as the Legislature may prescribe."

Although states have broad, overarching authority to develop, create and educate students, the federal government has also mandated that schools must seek to adequately educate each student. We saw this in President's Bush mandate entitled the "No Child Left Behind Act." Although state governments have broad education autonomy, it also must follow rules set forth by the federal government because of funding requirements. But ultimately, significant power remains with state governments to develop an educated population.

The fact remains states have large control over its education systems, and too many urban schools are under-educating its students. That said, maybe it's time for the federal judicial system to develop opinions and set mandates on this issue. Yes, this position may be somewhat radical, but what do we have to lose as a country. Integrating schools and desegregating social institutions also was a radical idea but look what happened. Have we experienced turmoil and setbacks as a country? Sure, we have. That's a part of the political and democratic process. So, I submit, the federal judiciary, particularly, the U.S. Supreme Court cannot afford to sit on the sidelines as urban schools continue to apply band-aids to this problem. Besides, the Supreme Court punted this issue in *Brown* II when it decided that local courts were best to accomplish the *Brown* I mandate. If states and urban schools won't fix this problem, maybe it's time for some version of *Brown* to be revisited.

Urban schools are guilty of conveying a false sense or impression that they are not to blame for the considerable woes urban students face after graduation. That's after considering the likelihood or possibility that the urban student graduates. The U.S. Constitution is not silent as to whether students must have a constitutional right to a public education, but silent as to this idea of an adequate education, thus what constitutes it as adequate. But the supreme court has fiercely defended public education, therefore we know that it is protected. But maybe urban schools can argue that this concept of adequacy within the education context is contextually based. What do I mean? What suburban schools consider as adequate may not be what urban schools consider what is adequate. Maybe urban schools have convinced themselves that we do the best with what we have. What they may or may not have encompasses adequate financial resources, classroom technology, great teachers, and parents that teach their students to value education.

Problem with that argument is it doesn't explain away my central argument that urban students are being deprived of an equal opportunity to achieve life, liberty, and property as articulated by the 14th amendment. Getting an education isn't just about getting books and grades. Getting an education isn't just about students leaving home for seven hours a day. Urban schools are pushing their students into what the 13th amendment has prohibited—involuntary servitude except for punishment to a crime. The first ten amendments are known as the bill of rights. They are effectually known as such because they are core to our democratic being and protects us from discriminatory forces and grants us many freedoms like a free public education and free speech.

As you engage this text, remember equal protection of the law to the 14th amendment and due process is the basis for the boastful claim that a constitutional crisis exists within the context of urban schools clashing with the 14th amendment. An adequate education may not be a fundamental right guaranteed by the constitution, but there is no denying that true life, liberty, and property is best achieved through the attainment of an adequate education. No life should be taken for granted but urban schools have proven that the principles embedded in the 14th amendment do not apply to urban students.

Let me be clear, I undoubtedly am aware that all urban schools are not guilty of my assertion. These are my opinions, assertions, claims based on my experience as a student, substitute teacher, parent, and mentor to urban students. As I always articulate, one student left behind is too many. That said, it is widely known that these schools permit to many urban students to fall through the cracks.

Chapter 1

Equal Protection Argument

I would argue that the U.S. Constitution is the second most important document following the bible. The constitution continues to be the most debated in social, political and intellectual circles across this nation. Its impact is widely known and understood. Similarly, to the bible, it contributes to shaping our better consciences in some respects. But ultimately, it is a significant guiding framework that contributes to a pluralistic governing society. It attempts to keep up with a society that is ever evolving to ensure that rights, privileges and opportunities are not abridged. That said, it's important to remember there is no one right way to interpret the constitution. What one person may believe should be protected by the constitution, someone else may take a different view. However, this is democracy at its best and it isn't cheap.

Some will argue that there isn't an equal protection argument to be made within the urban school context. And they are entitled to that position. I happen to think there is an argument to be made. Regardless of how tenuous the argument may seem, there is one to be made. Because I can't predict the future, I can't say that there is a judicial appetite to litigate the merits of equal protection within the urban school context in the future. However, that doesn't mean the discussion or debate should not be had.

The 14th amendment expresses as follow. All persons born or naturalized in the United States, and subject to the jurisdiction thereof, are citizens of the United States and of the State wherein they reside. No state shall make or enforce any law which shall abridge the privileges or immunities of citizens of the United States; nor shall any State deprive person of life, liberty, property without due process of law; nor deny to any person within its jurisdiction the equal protection of the laws.[2]

But what does it mean or what does it look like to not afford someone his equal protection of the law? Laws discriminate by imposing a burden on one person, while granting a special privilege or exemption to another person. In essence, the law chooses to disadvantage one person instead of another because of his race, ethnicity, gender, sexuality, religion, or etc. For example, a government entity has written and adopted a policy that permits only one African American male and female to be promoted to any supervisory position. Or take this example. A private company that receives government funding has instituted a policy that must hire one white person to every black hired. The policies have predetermined how many people can be hired depending on their race or gender without consideration to their qualifications. Such a policy may blatantly discriminate on its face. However, some policies are not discriminatory on its face and may not be written as law.

De facto policies are not written as law. A de facto law is governed by norms and behavior that dictate an environment. With a de facto law, there is implicit understanding by organizations or company leaders that a policy will be carried out although it is not written and adopted. Such laws are more difficult to prove. It is important to point out that de facto laws are only discriminatory if the unwritten policy or law is carried out by a government institution or a private company that receives or bids on government contracts, which is known as State Action. To that point, a Kroger or Walmart would not fall under the purview of judicial review if an equal protection charge was leveled. That said, that doesn't mean private companies can outright discriminate. The federal government has established federal agencies to hold private companies accountable depending on the violation. However, for the purposes of this book, an analogy is unnecessary.

In too many urban schools, educators have minimum or no expectations for too many students. The inference is that urban educators do not have minimum or no expectations for all its students. Society at large pre-determines what child will be successful depending on his gift. Referencing this point is important because urban schools are not just to blame for this phenomenon. Students that are considered prodigies receive more than special treatment. Students that are considered smart are grouped together. Student-athletes are often grouped with the smart students to keep them on the right path, or they are giving privileges that even smart students are not given. As a high school senior, I had to learn a 100-line stanza poem for one point to graduate. On the opposite end of the spectrum—a star athlete that had a B average received the same opportunity and got several points to earn an "A." Moreover, many urban student athletes are giving free pass from class and given unearned grades.

Back to my contention, the IQ of the student determines where the student is grouped. It determines if he gets a good or bad teacher. It determines if he receives advice or instruction from the school counselor. It determines if he can join any club or organizations. It determines if he is forced into special education, although the student does not meet the criteria. Essentially, the lower the urban student's perceived IQ, determines the level of adequate education received. However, it just isn't about IQ. It is also about a student with discipline problems. If a student struggles with behavior, there is no way to determine his or her intellect or capacity to learn. However, in too many urban schools, teachers or administrators adopt the notion that this isn't their problem. Their job is to do one thing—and that is to teach the kids that are ready and capable to learn.

I will hammer this point throughout the book. Urban schools cannot separate or dismiss sociodemographic challenges from what occurs in their schools because there structural and cultural challenges stem from it. An interesting article entitled "*Framing Urban School Challenges: The Problems to Examine When Implementing Response to Intervention*," takes a profound look into urban school culture and suggests ways to fix these schools.

The authors write in part. "Sociodemographics are not simply an artifact of urban education; rather, they have a significant impact on how urban schools are structured. The concentration of poverty and racial isolation matter in that it is directly related to school processes that significantly influence student achievement trends. The challenges of urban education cannot be divorced from its sociodemographic context. These challenges facing urban school systems have both structural and cultural components. Structural challenges are specific school policies and practices that impede student success or fail to adequately address students' needs. Alternatively, cultural challenges are those policies, practices, and sets of beliefs that contribute to dysfunctional perceptions of students' intellectual abilities—particularly those students who are culturally and linguistically diverse—due to limiting predictors of school achievement.[3]

Too often urban students are failed before rendered an academic opportunity. Urban schools have pre-determined based on grades and test scores if a student deserves a fair shot. I am not suggesting that all urban schools are guilty of this practice. But I am suggesting that such a policy is de facto. I strongly believe that this policy is culturally embedded in the fabric of urban schools that take this approach. I have a difficult time believing that school boards would sign off on policies that group students based on their perceived ability.

Remember, I defined and provided examples of equal protection violations. I explained that a violation may be found when one set of individuals are provided an opportunity, while some other group or individuals are disadvantaged or handed a special burden.

Here is the position from which I start my equal protection argument. Students that are perceived intellectually deficient are placed in conditions that make it unlikely or difficult they will academically succeed. These students are put into the worst teacher's classroom. They are not taught. Even, if the teacher desires to teach, the students make it difficult for one reason or another. Each student has his own set of challenges that makes the poor teachers' job difficult. Instead of the teacher developing a culture that invites academic growth and discipline—the teacher acts as a babysitter. In essence, the urban school creates an environment that suppresses struggling student's academic opportunity by failing to diversify classrooms.

However, down the hall, the classroom is filled with students that have shown an ability to learn and learn quickly. These urban students are put in effective teachers' classrooms because they have the best shot of making the teacher look good and providing the school with an opportunity to not be taking over by the state. While this strategy may seem effective because these schools managed to be labeled with a "C" or "D" just to keep state education leaders from taking over them, they bet against students with perceived limited academic ability. This is the very example of not treating all students the same that are similarly situated. These students come from similar home and community backgrounds, but urban schools treat them different because one student learns differently or quicker than the next student.

Recently, I was approached by a friend that experienced learning problems with her son. She was convinced that he could

Equal Protection Argument

learn but didn't know how to help him. Of course, he attended an urban school and the first suggestion they made was to put him in special education. After she disagreed, they attempted to force him into special education. Because she values education and just believed her son could learn, she sought out additional help by getting him tested. She learned that he was dyslexia. After she informed the school, the school also had him tested to confirm his disability. If you are like me, you are wondering why they didn't have him tested before mandating he be placed in special education. As you can see, urban schools are too comfortable finding the simple solutions to an urban students' problem besides going the extra mile. And because he had an academic disability, the school found it easier to place him in special education, instead of making sure he got an equal opportunity at the same education as his peers.

Undoubtedly, I am aware of the limited financial and human resources by urban schools. I also am aware that many urban schools just take a back-seat approach to urban students with perceived academic and behavioral problems, instead of investing in resources that will assist these students. It is no secret that many urban schools invest dollars in programs that are unnecessary only to pad pockets of persons they may have a relationship with. To that point, I am not naïve. I know every student can't be saved. But too many urban students are given a raw deal at an equal opportunity for an equal education.

Across the country, some urban school districts have garnered the nerves to fight for what is right. In Chicago, teachers went on strike seeking better pay, smaller classrooms, additional support staff and more increased funding for resources.[4] In Arizona, urban schools are challenged dealing with a significant number of kids living in poverty and lack home stability. Because of this fact, the school requires additional financial and human support to teach its students.[5]

So, my question to you, when does this type of systemic, unfair treatment end? When do more school systems step up and demand a better education system for their students as some school districts have done. I wrote this book to prick the better consciences of those that care or maybe think they shouldn't care. And it is my hope that college students studying to become teachers and new teachers approach urban education differently, rather than aligning with the status quo. All urban students deserve a chance, not just the ones with perceived potential. And as research has often suggested and proved, too many students that achieve in high school, can't seem to transition their high school classroom success to real life. Therefore, it's imperative that all urban student receive an equitable opportunity at life, liberty, and property.

Notes

Bill Shupe, www.centerforindividualism.org/the-real-story-of-the-college-admissions-scandal (March 2019).

The Bill of Rights Institute, www.billofrightsinstitute.org/founding-documents/constitution.

Roey Ahram, Adeyemi Stembridge, Edward Fergus, Pedro Noguera, "Framing Urban School Challenges: *The Problems to Examine When Implementing Response to Intervention (April 2019).*

Allison Stine, "Teacher Strikes Draw Attention to School-Family Connection," Caseygrant.org (March 2019).Ibid.

Chapter 2
My Story

I was raised by a beautiful, single mother named Diane McCullough. I had a brief relationship with my father until I was about nine, I presume, as many young black boys are all too familiar. It was just my mother, sister name Michelle, and I. My mother lived in my grandparent's house and sacrificed her life ambitions and educational endeavors to be the primary caretaker to her parents. My mother, sister, and aunt Jackie lived there at the time. The house had four bedrooms. That meant as early as I can remember, my sister and I shared a bed with my mother for some time. After aunt Jackie moved, I got my own room.

As a kid, I remember my mom taking courses at Tougaloo college. She never expressed why she failed to complete her course work, but as a single parent and caretaker to her parents, I understood how demanding life was for her. Great news, years later we both graduated together. I could not have been any prouder. I am fortunate to be raised by a strong woman with the help of other strong women that were her sisters. Their names are Cathy, Jackie, and Constance. The older I got, the more I understood that our family valued education. I was told my grandmother, Hattie, was an educator before she fell ill. My grandmother today is still ill and has been since I was a young boy. She is truly my inspiration.

In elementary, I was an honor student. I remember my mother spending countless hours helping me with homework and reading. But, after entering middle school, my grades took a sharp dive. Middle school was a very different beast. I guess I can blame many different factors for my academic decline. But I think first and foremost, in retrospect, it was the cruel and corrupt culture that existed in that school. The stories of Nichols Middle School preceded it with quite the reputation. If you were not used to protecting yourself, you had to quickly learn. The question was not are you going to get bullied, but when.

Picture the iconic movie "Lean on Me," and if you have any recollection of it, you have a true sense of my school environment. While in middle school in the early nineties, students were repeatedly failed and remained grades behind. I am not kidding when I say there were kids old as sixteen in the fifth or sixth grade. These older kids did only one thing well, bully. The sad part was, teachers use to deliberately leave the room minutes at a time, only to come back to one kid being beat down by an unsuspecting bully. If you ask me, the teachers were aware of what would occur in their absence.

I don't remember the time or day that I encountered my first bullying incident. But I did, and more than once. Mornings in middle school were particularly dangerous because kids ranging from fourth to seventh grade were all outside engaging in all types of raucous behavior. In fact, many fights would break out, even gang related. This was a dangerous and ideal time for bullies to prey on innocent fresh meat. But I was not bullied this way.

My first bully demanded my lunch money, and I said no. So, he told me that I was certain to get it. The teacher left out of the class and he punched me in back of the head. You better believe I was scared for my life. This kid was about six feet and weighed about two hundred pounds. I turned around, close my eyes and started swinging for his face. Less than a minute later, the teacher returned and broke up the fight. I didn't have any more problems that day forward with him. However, I experienced maybe four or five more bullying incidents with different bullies. After consistently fighting back, it became clear that I was not to be bullied.

Middle school became less about education, and more about survivor. In order to survive, being cool and defending yourself was the master recipe. When it comes to learning in middle school, much of it was a blur. There wasn't a teacher that inspired me. There wasn't a teacher that talked about the real world, and education being vitally important. I guess I could speculate why teachers did not take this approach to teaching, but I don't have any idea.

Fast forward to my eight-grade year, I just made it to high school. Most eight graders are still in middle school, but my high school started at eight-grade. At least now, I was well adjusted to the culture, and considered myself to be pretty cool, and equipped to defend myself. If you are waiting on a story about being a part of clubs and organizations that taught leadership, this is the wrong book. I don't want to mischaracterize my high school by saying there were no such clubs or organizations, but I was not aware of any. Moreover, teachers always chose who they desired to participate in those organizations. If we had student government, I am clueless as to what they did. I want to

My Story

be entirely clear; I am not saying that clubs and organizations did not exist. I am saying, I just wasn't aware.

In the classroom, I was a decent student. As I matriculated through many classes, I ended up in the worst teacher's classes with the most disruptive students. I had fun like the typical student in class or outside of it, but I never created chaos. I remember my math teacher literally drinking liquor in class. Yes, he got drunk, and this is not an exaggeration. As a result of having poor math instructors, the highest math I took was Algebra I. By the time I graduated, I lacked all necessary math skills to be successful in college.

As a student in high school my mother often worked two jobs, especially during the holidays. She was rarely there. She has always demonstrated the importance of hard work. She always made sure we had food, shelter, and nice attire. All that said, she just didn't have the time to make sure I was spending time studying, reading, and doing homework. But that is typical in black families with single mothers. Fathers get a pass on responsibility, while the mothers are left with the burden of raising kids on their own.

To say the very least, all I did was graduate. My senior year of high school, I remember earning six F's in seven classes during the first nine weeks. Not sure what I was doing, but it could have not been lesson. However, I managed to graduate 144 out of 167 students. Yes, I was at the bottom of the class, but I was just excited to graduate.

It was time for a decision to be made. Would I waste time trying to go to college with my horrible grades, or would I work?

My mother and aunts all made it clear that going to college was mandatory. They told me that a black man had no choice but to educate himself. Boy, were they, ever right? But the road has been long and hard to get to where I am today.

The first step was to seek a college that would accept someone with very unimpressive grades. I knew it would be a difficult task. I knew it, and my mother and aunt Cathy knew it; however, their faith told them different. This did not deter them, no matter how deterred I was. Years later I learned that when my mother contacted my high school to retrieve my transcript to submit as part of my college applications, the counselor told her I was not college material. She also said I would be better off finding a job. Who could blame her? I was even convinced that know school in its right mind would admit me.

My grades were so terrible, I applied to almost every junior college in Mississippi, and was denied. At that moment, I knew getting into a college or university would never happen. But, because of my mother operating off faith, she would not allow me to quit. I was denied by every black college and university in Mississippi. I was defeated. I began to look for employment. Unsure what my future would hold, I convinced myself college was not for me. All I could think, that counselor was right. All of a sudden, when hope was as dim as an outhouse with no lighting, to my disbelief and astonishment, Stillman College accepted me. Immediately, I thought to myself, this institution must be quite desperate for students.

After being admitted, I visited the school that summer for a few days and stayed on campus. I learned that the school was starting its first ever football team. I always desired to play high school football, but my mother didn't allow me because she believed it was too dangerous.

After going back home, I told my mom that I was trying out for the football team. She didn't really agree, but she knew it was my decision. I went back to start school a month early to tryout. When I arrived, I immediately knew I would not make the team because there were over four hundred young men trying out. Within that number, they had recruited several players from high school. I was devastated. It was no way I would make the team. After three days of competing, I learned that I made the team as a fourth stream running back and even made the special teams as a punt returner. This was the happiest day of my life. Now, it was time for classes to begin.

I can't quite remember my first day of class because it was mostly teachers introducing themselves, setting expectations, and outlining the semester. However, at some point, I quickly realized that I was not in high school anymore. I remember being in every class and thinking how these kids knew so much. I could not understand how they could process the information so quickly and express themselves so intelligently. Fear quickly set in, and I knew that the semester would be long and difficult.

I would prepare for class by reading but couldn't quite understand or retain the information. I could read the words on the pages, but I could not make inferences from what the author wrote. How could? I was never taught that. If I was taught it, I guess I missed class or classes that day. It was horrible. My self-confidence plummeted. I called home almost daily to cry and complain that I didn't belong in college and my peers were brilliant. I lacked discipline, consistency, study skills and good habits.

I accepted the notion that I was not college material, and it would be a matter of time before I was exposed as a fraud that couldn't read, analyze or think. So, I begun to party as much as possible, hung with friends, lift weights three to four times a day, and played football. I still went to class but halfway tried. I had convinced myself I was wasting my time. Well, at the end of the semester, I earned a stunning 1.67 grade point average and landed on academic probation. That meant I could only take a maximum of thirteen hours a semester until I pulled my grade point average up to a 2.0.

I went home and told my mother and aunt that I wasn't going back. I remember saying, what was the use. Immediately, they said let's pray. We prayed, but I didn't feel any better. They sat and told me stories about how they knew I was different from the time I was born, and they spoke over my life that I would someday become a successful attorney. I thought, good luck with that ever happening. I still wasn't convinced, so they reminded me why a black man had to be educated. I understood, but just didn't think I could muster my way through four years of college. So, they gave me a final ultimatum. Either you go back to school, or you find a job and somewhere to stay. Wow, I thought. I knew they were serious. After, the Christmas break, I went back to complete my second semester.

I convinced myself that I had the ability to do college level work. I went back to Stillman with a resolve and determination to do well. It was difficult, I must admit. I had to study many hours daily, and even dedicate my weekends. I had to learn to balance partying, social responsibility, and academics. I was not just working to maintain my grades; I also was trying to catch up to where the other students were academically. Without a doubt, my college peers were academically superior to me. I mean I played around my entire high school career, and even had several teachers that was only focused getting through the day, let alone, teaching. I won't say that students made their jobs easy because they didn't. But I believe, if you cannot handle your students, you have no business teaching.

All that said, I finished my second semester with a 2.2 grade point average. It wasn't enough to come off academic probation. It didn't matter because I had done something, I thought impossible. I thought what if I would have gone to a school district where academic excellence was a part of the culture, and more teachers gave a dam or saw potential in me. I even thought, what if I just had done a little more, regardless of the school culture, or the poor teachers that were there. Maybe if I would have shown more potential, teachers would have invested more in me. In that moment, I tried to convince myself that I failed me, not teachers. Many students are not interested in the education process for one reason or another. It doesn't matter why; it matters that they are there as sponges. What matters is that all teachers understand and work to motivate and inspire the students that seem not to be worth their time. The students that seem to be a lost cause and have a limited bright future. I was that student. But I have accomplished more than they could have imagined. This is the type of character and attitude teachers must have that teach in urban schools.

My new profound success had become contagious. I knew this was the tip of the iceberg. I knew I wanted more and could do more. After being bombarded by Army recruiters on campus daily, I decided to read a brochure and listen to his sales pitch. Surprisingly, I was intrigued to learn what the military could do, especially, how it could help pay for my college education. So, I believe it was May of 2000, I decided that I would join the Army Reserve. But I knew I needed my mother's consent. I remember when I went home and shared my idea to enter the Army, she asked "have you lost your mind." I replied, "no."

"I am serious mother; I want and need to do this for me."

"Well, it seems you have really thought about this, so I want get in your way."

"Crap," I thought.

I was hoping she would have stayed stern to her position. Now, I had to go through with it. It didn't matter. It was time for me to be about something other than myself. I needed a cause to support and defend. What better cause than to protect and serve Americans and this country's values.

That settled it, I called the recruiter that next day, and told him I was ready to commit and sign the necessary paperwork.

After taking the ASVAB, signing the necessary paperwork, passing the physical examination, I was off to Fort Knox, Kentucky for nine weeks of basic training. I could tell you that it was easy, but it wasn't. It wasn't easy getting up every morning at 4:30am and being dressed by 5:00 am to go through rigorous physical training. Most of the training was combat related. We ran four days a week, an average of 40 miles. From climbing trees, ropes, crawling in mud and water, while live artillery fired over my head, I thought a couple times, what in the heck have I signed up for. It didn't matter, I knew I couldn't quit. I was determined to complete basic training. Just nine weeks later, I completed training, and was a different man. At that moment, I felt indispensable and unbeatable. I took this approach back with me to college.

First day back on Stillman College campus as a second-year freshman due to an unsuccessful first year, but I was determined to achieve academic excellence this time around. That year I spent more time in the library, more time with my professors, and less time partying. Guess what! It paid off. That semester, I earned a 2.7 grade point average, and managed to come off academic probation. That was it. I had proved to myself and did what my mother and aunts knew I could do. Those grades solidified for me, I had the ability to not only think and write analytically, but I enjoyed the learning process. To improve my spoken and written communication, I began to read the dictionary daily, and use words I learned periodically in everyday written and spoken communication. You have no idea how thrilled I was. Professors and administrators begin to show me attention and to seek out even more to help me. Many of them said, "we believe you have a gift in writing, and you should think about majoring in English."

In 2003, I transferred to Tougaloo College, a historical

black college. While at Tougaloo, I began to really compete with some of the best and brightest. I had already proved to myself that I had the ability to be a good student. Now I focused on being the better student. Although it took me seven years to get my first degree in English, I did it. Not only did I get one degree, I earned a master's in public policy administration from Jackson State University in 2014, and a Juris Doctorate degree from Mississippi College School of Law in May 2017.

Years later my mother and I spoke about my formal education years while in middle and high school. We discussed the problems the schools faced then, and now. To that point, my mother and I talked about some teachers that clearly had no business in a classroom, and the overall culture of the school. She admits now that the culture didn't focus on academic progress or excellence and wishes she would have gotten me out of the school district. I told her I could have done some things different, and yes, I wish I could have possibly gone to a different school district. To be clear teachers and urban schools are not the only blame.

Because of my experience with urban schools, it has been the driving force behind this book. My experiences have fueled my passion to be a mentor and fueled my passion to help as many students as possible to see beyond their present predicaments, and to take ownership of their future. Educating and mentoring young people is a daily grind, and it drives me to tune out the critics, and the opposition because it isn't about what they believe. It's about doing what is right for all students regardless where they grow up and school they attend.

Chapter 3
Court Action 1

While you are reading this text, some urban student is being pushed out of a classroom for shooting a spitball at another student or shooting a piece of paper into a garbage can. Urban students are pushed into in-school suspension for minor infractions consistently. The student struggles with behavior because maybe his mother isn't disciplining him or maybe she works two jobs and doesn't have time. Or maybe he watches his mother being beat by her boyfriend after coming into her house intoxicated. There are varying factors that will support the boy's emotional and physical behavior. But urban schools can care less or fight for the necessary resources to help investigate problems of students with academic or behavioral problems. The result is simple. Either suspend the student for a minor infraction or send him to in-school suspension. Either way, he loses instructional time and gathers the feeling that no one understands his plight.

For one, I believe there is no perfect union, no perfect institution or perfect people. My assumption could not be any right than now. This country's current political woes under President Trump's failed and disastrous leadership highlights this very fact. This is surmised idealism at its best. But I am not talking about a perfect union or a perfect people. I am talking about fairness at its core. Fairness for the urban students and families that are deprived of serious opportunity. If one thing is certain, most of this country's progress has come by way of federal court mandates. Social progress has come by way of bold political leaders, community leaders, attorneys, and federal court judges that believed the time for social progress was upon them. I believe we are at this critical juncture again. I believe the federal courts, particularly, the highest Court in the land is required to forge the type of educational progress needed to precipitate educational fairness in urban schools by mandating another version of *Brown*.

Here is Justice Thurgood Marshall dissenting on this very issue in *San Antonio Independent School District v. Rodriguez*. He writes, "the majority's holding can only be seen as a retreat from our historic commitment to equality of educational opportunity and as unsupportable acquiescence in a system which deprives children in their earliest years of the chance to reach their full potential as citizens. The Court does this despite any substantial justification for a scheme which arbitrarily channels educational resources in accordance with the fortuity of the amount of taxable wealth within each district."[4]

One of the great reformers I will repeatedly referenced, Dr. King, expressed how blacks began to see themselves as worthy of social progress. He writes."A second factor that has caused the [Black's] new self-Consciousness has been rapid educational advance. Over the years there has been a steady decline of crippling illiteracy. At the emancipation only, five percent of [blacks] were literate; today more than ninety-five percent are literate. Constant streams of [Black] students are finishing colleges and universities every year. More than sixteen hundred [Blacks] have received the highest academic degree bestowed by an American university. These educational advances have naturally broadened his thinking. They have given the [black] not only a larger view of the world, but also a larger view of himself."[5]

King's latter statement rings volume. This idea of a black a man seeing himself differently. Not only seeing himself different, but understanding education was fundamental to his new psychological state and his ability to do more than just merely exist, but to add value to his life and community. Along the way many blacks have lost this idea of self-worth, independent thought, and an unyielding willingness and passion to succeed. However, the black man doesn't just wake up and decide to think such a way. No, it begins with lack of education. It begins in the classroom. It begins in the hallways. It begins on the basketball court or football field. It begins with administrators and teachers being more than rulers of young people. No, it begins with their insistence that failure isn't an option. It begins with urban schools teaching urban students that sometimes and even often unfair and evil unconstitutional forces can impede and obstruct black social, economic and political progress does exist. It begins with urban institutions viewing urban education as a fundamental right. These are the conversations that black administrators and teachers must have. Not just have, but be embedded in the curriculum, or at the very least, the culture.

However urban schools have repeatedly shown its true color. It has repeatedly revealed that it refuses to adopt a pro-education and pro-evolution agenda and movement to move urban students in the direction of gaining a quality education. According to the *Journal of Blacks in Higher Education*, the nationwide college graduation rate for black students stands at an appallingly low rate of 42 percent. This figure is 20 percentage points below the 62 percent rate for white students."

Blacks are not just minority in population, but minority in post-secondary education attainment, adequate high school education, income, adequate health, home ownership and the list can extend beyond these listed. The time for court action is now. The time spent on the sideline watching selfish urban schools jeopardize young people's future must come to an end now, not tomorrow.

The late great Justice Thurgood Marshall was a leading pioneer in passing *Brown v. Board of Education*. The Justices of the highest court in the land ultimately decided that separate but equal is inherently discriminatory on its face. We may not be fighting against racism and bigotry that was at the heart of separate but equal policies, but it's time to fight for fundamental fairness in urban education for urban students. Where you live shouldn't be the sticking point to determine how adequate a high school education a student receives. The arguments before the Supreme Court of the highest land would be no different than they were fifty plus years ago. It is now time for *Brown*, part III in some shape, form, fashion, or capacity. This nation can no longer afford to tie its own hands and sit on them. This nation must choose to unshackle itself from the stain of egregious urban school education. I am a product of the urban school and the harbored disdain is legitimate. I didn't ask to feel this way about urban institutions—I had no choice. I was duped out of a quality education. I was duped out of securing and enjoying the American dream sooner. Certain urban teachers took for granted my education. They played Russian roulette without concern for my genuine welfare. But still I rise, I rose from the depths of mis and under-education.

Follow me for a minute as I argue for an adequate education for students that attend urban schools. I ask that you grant me this moment in time because I best am able to speak from first-hand knowledge what occurs in urban institutions. As I express why these students deserve an adequate education, imagine I am in the United States Supreme Court arguing the merits of this case before the nine Justices of the Supreme Court. Before arguing the merits, I will briefly name and mention some important points and facts about the justices and their roles.

The Justices are Justice Samuel Alito (Republican Appointed), Chief Justice John Roberts (Republican Appointed), Justice Clarence Thomas (Republican Appointed), Justice Anthony Kennedy (Republican Appointed), Justice Neil Gorsuch (Republican Appointed), Justice Sonia Sotomayor (Democratic (Appointed), Justice Elena Kagan (Democratic Appointed), Justice Ruth Bader Ginsburg (Democratic Appointed), and Justice Stephen Breyer (Democratic Appointed).

I think it is important to quickly point out that although these

Justices are considered to be non-partisan—their opinions over the years on cases renders insight into their political affiliations, as well as the Presidents that have appointed them. By that analogy, it seems that there are five Justices with Republican ideology and four with democratic leaning principles. But there is one republic appointed Justice that sometimes find himself siding with Democrats. He has been considered a swing vote in many pivotal and controversy cases, and that is Justice Kennedy. I make this point because if I have any chance in persuading this court that urban school students deserve an adequate and fair education, Justice Kennedy likely will be that critical vote needed to win. As a very important side note, Justice Anthony Kennedy has retired, and Judge Brett Kavanaugh has been nominated to succeed Kennedy. When he is confirmed, this changes the political dynamics of the court and will certainly threaten any hope that the Supreme Court will have to ever recognize public education as a fundamental freedom.

As I make the difficult walk gasping for breath—a walk that seemed unending, my heart raced with fear, but not your typical fear. This wasn't a fear of public speaking or a fear of unpreparedness. No, I put every ounce of my being into preparing for this moment. This fear stems from possible failure or an inability to prick the hearts and minds of at least five Justices that are needed to forge a new path for urban education in this country. While making the climb to the top to reach the brass doors to the Supreme Court, I repeatedly replayed my opening statement in my mind. One more dry rehearsal I silently thought. "Urban school students are the recipients of educational neglect, unfair educational treatment, and discriminatory education policies that fails to promote a progressive education agenda that take into account urban students varying backgrounds and socio-economic challenges. I am not referring to obvious discriminatory policies that are unfair based on race, but education policies that intentionally mis-educate and under-educate the urban student." I am convinced that these are the introductory words needed to immediately paint a compelling, dire picture to this court in order to grab their attention. I have only one shot to possibly changed the trajectory and landscape of urban education, so I had to bring my "A" game. The stakes were enormous, and the future beneficiaries depends on me—at least I have convinced myself.

Ladies and Gentlemen of this prestigious body, "May It Please the Court." Members of this esteem and distinguished institution, I stand before you today, not just as an attorney (Petitioner) or advocate. No, I stand before you as a concern citizen, parent, and a product of an urban school system. A system that deliberately chooses not to protect the most vulnerable students in our society. A system that pretends it isn't conscious of the super need to promote education differently. An adequate and fair education for all students that isn't based on politics, based on economic status, based on where a student resides. No, I proclaim none of these things shall matter. This isn't just about the state of public education in urban schools. This is about fairness and human decency. This is about protecting what the 14th amendment to the U.S. Constitution embodies and promises to all citizens of this great union. This is about saving democracy and promoting capitalism for all. I urge you each to keep the 14th amendment in mind and the rights that succeeds from it as I argue why an adequate education should be fundamentally fair in this country.

The 14th amendment focuses on fundamental fairness regardless of race. It also protects a fundamental interest of liberty to pursue happiness. Happiness is a vague term that we often associate with the concept of achieving personal goals and ambitions. The 14th amendment also guarantees the right to challenge policies (due process) against certain fundamental rights. This fundamental right to challenge what is perceived wrong or is actually wrong is what makes our union so different and beautiful at the same time. This ability to challenge what seems to be less-democratic principles is what sets this great nation a part and convinces other nations to follow our lead.

Under the Constitution, public education is not a fundamental right; however, if a state builds a school, all students must be granted access to that school without any restrictive requirements. However, I would argue that an adequate education is also a fundamental right. Schools must go beyond public-school access. Public schools have an intimate responsibility to adequate educate its students. Here lies the issue with too many urban schools. To that point, I stand before this Court to challenge the constitutionality of consistent, inadequate urban-school education policies that have under-educated, mis-educated and misguided these students for too long. I contend that one reason why urban school's failures continue to slip through the crack is because the perception is that state's education school boards pretend to hold urban schools accountable. I also contend that urban schools continue down the path of failing urban students because of traditional, outdated educational practices.

    These education policies that don't address urban student's needs are shameful and a disgrace. These schools are teaching to the test. These schools are hiring less than adequate teachers. These schools are giving grades to athletes that ultimately hurts him. These schools quickly punish behavior with too many days away from the education process. These schools place too much blame on the parents, after the parents have made clear their intentions not to help their students engage the education process. These schools are known for doing a poor job at eradicating a culture of academic failure. These schools group kids based on their academic performance. These schools have too large of a class, so good teachers struggle to effectively reach their students. These schools are not teaching students the importance of social and civic engagement. These schools are not establishing certain clubs and organizations that will help the student see beyond their understanding of the larger world. These schools are not exposing these students to a culture outside of their communities. These schools are not having the critical conversations necessary to educate the urban student about the less than flattering institutions that will seek his life unfairly. I understand how this may sounds. I understand the message or signal it may send to the nation. But excuse me, I am not here to express what is politically polite or correct—no I am here to intensely shine a light on a problem that is stage four cancerous. These schools neglect to teach these students how to independently think. These schools fail to establish lines of communication between teachers and students. Yes, these are intentional acts that amount to a serious miscarriage of educational justice.

It is not okay to treat urban students like cattle. This is not slavery where owners sold off men, women, and children as though they were non-liked, unloved, and uncared for by love ones. This country needs to recognize the damage urban schools are causing innocent urban youth. Urban youth have no control of their circumstances and because of urban schools—it seems as they have no control of their own future. Think about it. They are born into a system that has cast a net over any potential they may have. Their dreams, hopes, and ambitions are subdued by urban education's inadequacies. This is more than just race we are talking about. Sure, black students are a large subset of the population I am referring to, but this isn't a "Black Lives Matter Movement." This is an urban student's live movement. A movement, Justice Thomas that deserves considerable attention. This is why I stand before you today. I am fearful if the highest court in the land doesn't step in, urban schools will continue down a path of devastation and destruction.

We are a nation of laws, but we also are a nation that depends on lawlessness. What an interesting paradox? Is it absurd to say that we depend on lawlessness, maybe, but these are not normal times? We live in a society where we punish crimes in my judgment entirely too harsh. We have outsourced many of our public prisons to the private sector. We tell the American public that it helps states save tax dollars. We tell the American public that the state doesn't have the human and capital resources to manage jails and the influx of criminals. But, in reality, the private system complex is a money-making machine and scheme. A machine that depends on criminals. But, have we thought, where most of these criminals come from? Do we seriously believe that they come from our richest, suburban communities and schools? Do we seriously believe they come from our private schools where one hundred percent of students attend college? Of course not. We dam well know where these students come from. The prison-to-pipeline system is real.

It doesn't matter. We say that parents need to step up. What about the social dynamics that parents cannot change? Many urban parents grow up in poverty-stricken areas working sometimes two and three jobs. However, we expect urban parents to raise kids that they literally don't have time to see. Am I making excuses for less involved parents, of course not? I am stating the facts. We can choose to accept it or not. Is it their fault that they must work more than one minimum wage job? I imagine not. This society we live can care less about students that grow up in poverty and attend poor public urban schools. This is the real American travesty. We bet against urban student's success to capitalize on the private prison system complex.

In 2002, President George W. Bush passed into law the "No Child Left Behind Act." Americans praised the decision. Rightly so, if you ask me. We all knew that American students were behind the curve in education in comparison to countries like India, Japan, Korea and China. However, that fact still remains true today. After a few years of the new law, teachers realized that the law was only designed to prepare students for more exams than necessary. The law was an utter and epic failure. To this point, it has always blown my mind that suburban schools were never labeled as failing but forced to change its education policies. These schools didn't need no child left behind. This law was targeted to address the needs of the urban public school. In short, the urban public school began to focus on teaching to the test, instead of teaching the student. I should know, I was required to teach the test to my students and witnessed my cohorts do the same.

I have articulated my impassioned plea today why education policies in urban public schools must change. I am certain that it must be a mandate from this court. Do I believe in humanity, definitely? Do I trust these schools to do right by these students, of course not? These schools must be forced to holistically address all urban student's need. Is this vague, sure, but these schools must take a student-center approach that investigates why the urban student rebels against the education process. These schools must investigate why urban students repeatedly engages in misconduct. These schools must investigate why the urban student repeatedly interrupts the education process. These schools must investigate the urban student's home environment to get an understanding of the student's philosophy on academic responsibility, or a lack thereof.

Justices of this Court, I am not asking you to do the politician's job or the school system's job. No, that would be absurd. I'm asking you to recognize *Brown* never reached its intended policy goals. We have different branches of government for a reason, and I whole-heartedly believe in the integrity of these institutions. But that does not erase or eradicate the power of this court. You have the ability to force states to implement laws. At the very least, I am seeking a broad mandate that does not compel these schools but requires these schools to change the way they educate students from distressed communities. I ask this court to think about solving this problem with some variation of a *Brown*.

You recently took two bold actions under President Obama's administration. You made it the law of the land that all U.S. citizens must purchase health insurance or be penalized. Second, you passed same sex marriage. Two hot button, and hotly contested issues that has plagued this country for years. With high regard for this court, I would argue that politically the people of this great nation spoke and made clear that it was time to give same-sex couples the same rights as heterosexual couples and healthcare was a right, not a privilege. Was it easy? Of course not. But was it right, I contend yes? You saw this issue as more than a human right, but a civil and fundamental right as this Court has viewed many critical issues to advance laws that have moved this country forward. I ask you to be on the right side of history as this Court has demonstrated time and time again.

Today's issue concerning these types of public schools are no different. Education reform is a serious civil right that must be confronted. While politicians are entrenched in political rhetoric that serves no genuine purpose, student's lives are being dismantle. The United States Congress and its Department of

Education has made it clear that it will not supersede the power of the states. It is also important that they cannot without states suing for an injunction, but this body has great latitude to change the direction of urban school's direction. It has been repeatedly proven that state legislatures refuse to do what is right for struggling urban schools that unfortunately includes too many minorities. Inadequate funding and teacher attrition are constant. That said, politicians consistently make campaign promises that center around social change and social fairness. I would argue, what social change is more important than adequately educating our most vulnerable. We are one of the richest countries in the world, yet, we have significant poverty, homelessness, and schools where kid's future is stolen daily.

As a country we talk about these critical issues that plague America, but at the heart of solving it requires focusing on an adequate education for all Americans and not a few. Case and point, the U.S. Secretary of Education, Bessie Devos, was interviewed in February of 2018 about the significant number of failing urban schools, and what ideas did she have to combat the issues urban schools face. She immediately expressed the need for more charter schools to compete against urban schools. I think there is some merit to this argument, but what caught my immediate attention was when Ms. Devos was asked had she ever visited these schools, her response, "No I have not." Allow that to sink in for a moment.

The highest education official in the United States, who job is to develop, design, implement policy and work with departments of education around the country to see what policies would work better in public schools has failed at the most basic level.

This is an American travesty. Economics and where you live should not determine how much success you will acquire in life. This is fundamentally unfair, just like separate but equal was inherently unequal, unfair and unjust. If this Court does not step in, our American democracy is in jeopardy. Democracy should spread vast and wide. I earnestly ask you to open up the floodgates of democracy because it isn't only the sensible thing to do, but the right thing. Democracy too should not be tied to economics, but American capitalism has forgotten about the masses, and refuses to adopt some form of populism. These students deserve better and have been failed for too long.

In closing, I am asking this honorable Court to make the right decision. This may be an unprecedented request, but these are unprecedented times that requires unorthodox intervention. Ask yourself this pressing question? Fifty years from now—what do you want history books to say about you. Are you willing to relinquish your opportunity to make history? I sure hope not. Recently, you made history by granting same-sex couples the right to marry. I am pleading with you to not turn a deaf ear or a blind eye to this public crisis. Only this Court has the ability to change the social, cultural, and political narrative and conditions around urban public education. I am asking you to do what is only right, and to help protect democracy and urban student's futures.

Chapter 4
A Constitutional Crisis

He walked into my office, an ex-urban student—and as we talked more, I learned he was an ex-inmate. I was all too familiar with the dialogue we were about to share.

He spoke. "Bruh, I just got out of the county and did two years for some weed charges. The weed wasn't even mines."

I thought, the American justice system targets young black men disproportionately than any other race. But, what could I say, but nod in full, incomprehensible agreement or say I feel you because I have been targeted on several occasions? I was at least half-lucky, I thought.

At least I was educated and knew if I stayed the course, my break would manifest itself someday. However, I would still remain a target for law enforcement. He talked for a few minutes about how the police was wack and how all his homeboys had either done time or were still doing time.

I felt his uncontrollable, silent need for attention or at least an unavoidable answer I couldn't give. But I could relate. I own a tax office, so it was first nature for ex-inmates to come to file old tax returns from any income earned before doing time—

hoping to score some quick revenue. I guess they came to me first because my office was less than a mile from the jail, and other inmates had told them that I was one of them.

What did they mean by one of them?

They meant that I came off as a real brother that understood their unfortunate plight and would help them in anyway, if possible.

He spoke about all the horrors of being incarcerated and promised himself that he would not go back. He promised himself that he would get a job and stay on a narrow path. This was common rhetoric among ex-inmates, I encountered. I truly wanted to believe each of them, but I knew the odds were slim. Recidivism was real. The next time I saw him would be a couple years later.

He walked in. I asked, "where have you been man?"

"Them folks got me again."

I couldn't say, I told you so, but I had encountered his kind too often. All I could say, "I hope you can get it together this time and let me know if I can help you.

He responded, "bet."

Bet in urban communities means, I will, or I appreciate it.

A couple weeks later, a few high school classmates of mine met at one of our usually spots. The night would be uncharacteristically humid—but this was Mississippi. There isn't much in Mississippi that is ever considered uncharacteristic since many things that are considered normal—may not be as normal in other parts of the country. That said, I digress to steer this discourse back where it was heading. As I was saying, my classmates and I were sitting outside on the patio at this very nice hotel that we frequented often to get away from Mississippi's social, political, cultural and economic miscues as we saw them. It was a place to engage serious issues of the day, but also a place to just wind down with a stiff drink and to watch a good game. This unsuspecting night we abandoned the chance to watch a game for some political talk. At this point, my partners were aware that I was writing this book and would often ask me how it was coming. I will reframe from using real names, so I will call them Paul and Chester.

As usual Chester liked to here himself talk and, on this night, he expressed why he believed urban schools were less to blame than I have premised this book.

I responded, "interesting, please give me your thoughts."

Besides I didn't want to be too far off base with my theory—and I have this pressing belief that many people will likely think that my rhetoric possibly goes too far or unfairly blames urban schools. That said, great, because maybe this book will acquire the necessary and proper attention.

"I had to ask him again to give me his reasoning," because of my repeated interferences.

Chester spoke.

"I am a product of an urban school as you are."

"Okay, now what is your point.?

"My point is you went off to school and now you have three degrees, and you are a product of an urban school."

I responded, "true."

"So, my point is simple, it comes down to individual choices even if you don't have a proactive parent that helps you see the value in education or if you attend an urban school."

I thought, momentarily. Not how I would respond, but the mere fact he believed the solution was that simple.

"WOW!!"

"You can't seriously think it's that simple, please tell me."

Chester replied, "I do."

He followed up that response with, "what do you think is the problem?

"Clearly you have not been listening to me as I have expressed many times why I have chosen to write this book."

However, Chester.

The real problem is not individual choice and responsibility. The real issue is urban schools and the established culture. Before you articulate parents must do more, I agree and disagree.

He responded, "please clarify both statements."

"Okay, this is what I mean." "Urban schools have a tendency to make the obvious and faulty assumption that urban students are aware of the importance of education. They make the faulty assumption that urban students come to school baggage free. They make the faulty assumption that it is impossible that an urban student just worked eight hours last night because she knows her mother or grandmother needs help to keep the lights on. Urban schools make the faulty assumption that urban students are exposed to the world outside of urban distressed communities. They make the faulty assumption that urban students ate last night or was able to acquire the adequate sleep necessary the night before. Urban schools make the faulty assumption that an urban student has even just one role model or mentor to model what success looks like".

He replied. "Okay, you have said a lot, but what does all that mean?"

"It means that urban schools must stop taking urban student's education for granted. It means that they must take a student-centered approach to educating urban students with their socio-economic issues in mind. It means they must focus on more than academics and develop a culture that focuses on the value of education—and a culture that identifies real world issues that many urban students will face after graduation." He pretended as he understood but remained emphatic that individual choice and responsibility was a culprit as well. It was clear that he just didn't get it. That was okay because I imagine many people will not get it or refuse to see my arguments as valid or even reasonable. There are many individuals a part of this great republic that hold outdated views that are no longer part of mainstream rhetoric. We still do not suppress their speech. The 1st amendment tolerates and permits wide ranging speech—even speech that symbolizes and borders hate. This is because we live in a pluralistic, democratic society with varying principles and belief systems. This is what makes this country so great. We can disagree to agree and hopefully find common ground.

A Constitutional Crisis

"*Push Out*," is an expressive book about urban schools, communities and the girls that come from them. Monique Morris writes, "My name is Danisha, and I'm eleven years old, and I'm a ho, that's what I do.... In some communities, girls learn early on that selling "fruit cocktail" is one of the few options they have to escape poverty. It's an idea effortlessly absorbed by the psyche of young girls from the moment they can play patty cake. Darnisha should have been telling us about her teachers or her fifth-grade homework; instead, she was describing her sex hustle. As you can see, tragedies surrounding urban schools and its communities are not restrictive to only young men. This crisis is not the least gender neutral, but seemingly color specific.

These are real stories of real students who are failed considerably and consistently by urban schools. This isn't some made up fantasy. Who would fantasize such? This is what a constitutional crisis resembles in real life. It is one thing to articulate what the 14th amendment expresses and implies, but another, to witness first-hand the horrors of urban students being victims of urban school's assault on the 14th amendment. "Separate remains unequal as schools with concentrated poverty and racial segregation are still likely to have less-experienced teachers, high levels of teacher turnover, inadequate facilities, and fewer classroom resources.... As options for desegregation have been curtailed by court rulings, the number of intensely segregated schools with zero to 10 percent white enrollment has more than tripled.... Students are once again predominantly assigned to schools based on where they live, and to the extent that neighborhoods are segregated, the schools remain so."[6]

According to recent research by the Center for American Progress, 70% of the country thinks more needs to be done to integrate high and low-poverty schools. "School integration is not just an ideal; it remains a difficult but essential means to creating equal opportunity for all children. Advocates who are serious about school integration should consider pursuing all strategies at their disposal, including consolidating regional school systems that make it possible to integrate schools at scale."[7] This brings me to the essential point made in my introduction—that is, a *Brown* III is needed to reduce urban schools assault on the 14th amendment. I believe many Americans are genuinely ready to support this idea. This point is important because it will help avert the constitutional crisis that exist in many states that have established urban schools that continue to assault and clash with the 14th amendment.

As I mentioned earlier, I indicated that a constitutional crisis exists when government fails to execute its proper duties in the process of carrying out processes and procedures to achieve some objective or social policy goal. If you think about the overarching goal of your state's constitution and our U.S. Constitution, the objective is to achieve some social goal. Think about the 2nd amendment and the right to bear arms or the 1st amendment and the protection it grants to exercise uninhibited free speech—and the freedom to exercise one's religion without government interference—and your right to freely and peacefully assemble and petition for or against ideas you value as socially significant. Public schools are absent of constitutions but are considered local governments in many districts. However, although they have strong autonomy—they must report to local and state governing boards. I guess you are wondering what's my point. My point is that urban schools and their governing bodies that oversee them are complicit in creating a constitutional crisis. All that said, the thrust of this book is about urban school's assault and clash with the 14th amendment and to adequately characterize how these schools are culprits of my claim.

After *Brown* passed in 1954, essentially overturning what *Plessy v. Ferguson* instituted as separate but equal, a *Brown* part II was necessary to review the process and progress that had been done to carry out desegregating public schools especially in the south. According to Michael Klarman, "although there was prompt compliance with *Brown* in the District of Columbia and some border states, the initial response in the Deep South was massive resistance…. For political and personal reasons, school board members resisted prompt and effective action toward desegregation [because] for example, many officials lived in communities that were staunchly opposed to desegregation [thus] would make them the focal point of segregationist pressure.[8]

Almost sixty years later, these schools are still segregated. But what we have now are de facto institutional practices that have persisted to permit public schools to remain segregated. After *Brown* passed its mandate forcing schools to desegregate—whites resisted vehemently while working fiercely to establish private schools to skirt the federal mandate. Although, integration did occur in some parts of the country, many jurisdictions were able to circumvent the law because of their ambition to set up private schools quickly as possible. And where jurisdictions were not able to avoid the mandate, white flight occurred. White flight is a process by which white people moved into suburbs to escape minorities and to continue the push for segregated schools. When we talk about residential segregation, we find there is a direct and implicit linkage to race and class. No one argues that income matters when seeking a home, but we can't overlook the way lines were drawn to reduce the number of minorities that white students would be exposed to. Daria Roithmayr, in her book, *Reproducing Racism: How Everyday Choices Lock in White Advantage*, she reminds us of that exclusionary history.

She writes. In a crucial historical moment that would pave the way for the rest of the country, the [Chicago Real Estate Board] put in place an ethics code provision that prohibit-ed brokers from selling to buyers who threatened to disrupt the racial composition of the neighborhood. The move was so effective that the National Association of Real Estate Board (NAREB) adopted an identical provision. Now brokers would have to risk their careers to sell across racial lines—state commissions were authorized by state law to revoke the state licenses of those brokers who violated this provision.[9]

The significance of this history is important because although whites and other institutional mechanisms used by them allowed this obvious pervasive behavior to persist to evade desegregation—urban schools are predominantly minority. This fact cannot be denied that urban schools have strong records of failing urban students. Aside from this country not achieving adequate integration, urban schools have shouldered the burden and struggled to adequate educate urban students. As such, urban schools have normalized failing urban students. The danger in this sort of normalization is recorded and identifiable. Year after year, urban schools have the same conversations and employ the same tactics to try to reduce its failed educational recidivism. I used the term recidivism just to show that urban schools are repeat offenders of the same policies and programs that have proven ineffective. As a result, failing urban schools help spread this narrative of "Black Exceptionalism."

What is it? At its core, black exceptionalism is a concept that purports that blacks, particularly men and boys, fare more poorly than any other group in the United States. This concept focuses on the notion that black men are not less capable or intellectually inferior, but the black male species faces greater social, political and economic burdens and challenges than others. This fact alone has created an emergence of organizations that focus their attention and resources to help black males circumvent systemic systems of unfairness. A Study conducted by Paul Butler takes a look into this phenomenon.

He writes in part. Many policy makers and scholars argue that, in fashioning racial justice strategies, we should treat Black males as a distinct group, separate and apart from Black women and other men. Motivating this idea is the view that African American men need special attention because they face unique circumstances and problems.... The claim is that by almost every index of inequality, Black males are on the bottom— exceptionally burdened and marginalized. For example, in an amicus brief in *Fisher v. Texas*, a coalition of "Black male achievement" organizations acknowledged that many young

Americans other than Black male youth face serious life course obstacles in need of attention, but ... the depth and breadth of negative life outcomes experienced by Black males are sufficiently grave to warrant independent investigation and policy prescription.... A diverse of organizations has responded to black male exceptionalism's appeal [and] has become a million-dollar industry.... In this respect, Black male exceptionalism has currency both ideologically and economically, structuring not only how we frame civil rights Interventions but how we fund them.[10]

Unfortunately, Black exceptionalism is a tangible thing in Black America. Urban schools bear the brunt of the blame because miseducation and undereducation has been normalized by urban schools, which means that urban communities suffer. For young urban males and females that strive to this idea of Black exceptionalism, it isn't an easy feat to defeat in many cases. My personal journey was difficult even outside of trying to navigate the academic rigors of college life. As an up and coming educated black man from an urban community, I had to learn to balance my new profound passion for learning and information. There were many instances my peers told me not to talk like that around them, or don't ever think you are better than the next person, or don't forget where you come from, or don't come around me with that white talk. Often, many ex-urban students that attempt to rise from the depths of urban-phycological thinking that is cemented in this idea of what black Americans should look and act like is a difficult transition to conquer. Ex-urban students can struggle with being "real," labeled as an outcast, or making the difficult and horrendous decision to completely separate herself from a community of individuals that do not share her value system of life any longer. Why this insistence that urban schools are the blame? Urban schools cannot reflect urban communities. Urban schools can't permit urban students to settle for what they just see in everyday life. They must be exposed emotionally and physically to Black exceptionalism. This behavior must be modeled for them in urban schools as frequently as possible to combat what they undoubtedly will witness in urban communities. This may mean carving out more time to allow them to role play their role in society as an educated black man or woman, and the responsibility that comes with it. It may require teachers and administrators finding ways to raise money or allocating money towards trips that will help shape and mold their way of thinking that reflects Black Exceptionalism. It may require time away from the classroom where an ex-urban student comes back and speak to urban students about the challenges he or she will face, but also about how it is doable with the right value system, hard work, and exercising delayed gratification. All these things are capable of being done, but instead urban schools ride down this rabbit trail of teaching to the test or teaching academic concepts—when urban students need exposure that will teach life lessons and how they are to fit and adapt to that life.

Let me be clear, I am not minimizing the process of education—I'm simply saying that teaching urban students seven hours a day is like life for many church goers that hear and read the word, but still fails to abide by God's principles. Think of it this way, Faith without Works is dead. Urban schools have too much faith in their current processes, when more work is needed to transform minds, attitudes and perceptions of urban students. If urban schools choose not to, urban communities will continue to choke hold the dreams and ambitions of urban students. As a result, urban communities will continue down a path of pervasive and corrupt bankruptcy—depriving urban students of opportunities that they at least once imagined; one can only assume.

Editor, Lerone Bennet, Jr. writes in a letter that the "institutions of American society have been systematically and mercilessly manipulated to keep [the Black man] down.... Bennet believes that there is an organized conspiracy against Black masculinity but "I won't entertain this argument because I believe the premise of my book demands my rhetorical silence.[11] That said, urban schools assault on the 14th amendment isn't just a brazen assertion to feed a redundant narrative that these schools continually and systematically fail urban students at alarming rates—no I submit this book is much more than what you see or understand on the surface or what is depicted in the media. This book is about painting a detrimental picture to the reader that these schools aren't just mis-educating and under-educating urban students but are adding to this narrative that across the board minorities are socially insignificant. Think about that assumption for a moment. Minorities are socially insignificant. The argument sounds like this—if they don't give a dam about their own, why should we. Bold statement and assumption but this must be the type of mindset and ideological thinking that urban schools must adopt to change gears from what is perceived as a very indifferent approach to urban student's future.

There seems to be this illogical assumption and loose thinking that this problem will fix itself. It seems that urban schools believe that urban communities are not an extension of urban schools and vice versa. This last statement should be a truism, but I am not so sure that it is. Just maybe urban schools believe that it sits on an island isolated from the social, political and economic problems that urban communities face. According to a study conducted in 2001 by Neild and Balfanz, "many urban students attend neighborhood high schools because these institutions are often characterized by chronic absenteeism, high dropout rates, widespread course failure, and low academic achievement...." Urban schools are also likely to be staffed by academically underprepared and inexperienced teachers and experience higher teacher turnover [and] in order for reform efforts to succeed, they will need sufficient intensity to address the substantial educational needs in [urban] schools.[12] Urban Schools have only two choices. The first choice is to develop and invest in programs that educate parents how to play a proactive role in their urban student's life, and the positive effect it will have. Or the second option is for urban schools to take up the slack where parents are failing. I toss this idea around a considerable amount in this book because I think this approach is more practical than the first choice. That said, schools must be held accountable regardless if parents and surrogate parents are failing to take a proactive role in their student's education. I can imagine many heads and eyes are rolling, but I fiercely stand by this belief, and will until some urban school proves me wrong.

If you think about it, it is no difference than what charter schools prescribe as the solution to reach, teach, and educate urban students from low and socio-economic backgrounds. It is all about culture, philosophy, and the way urban students value education. I continue to rack my brain around why do charter schools exist because if the idea behind them are autonomy, why not grant urban schools the same latitude and flexibility, especially when it has been proven that many charter schools experience academic success. Charter schools exist because someone or a group of individuals saw a need or an opportunity to develop one, thus create a vision and start with a mission. Each member is mission-driven, and everyone associated with the school knows what it stands for and believes in its vision. The school engages parents as real partners and fosters a culture that is highly collegial and focuses on continuous improvement. Each effective charter school has a strong accountability system and focuses on pleasing their clients—the parents and students.

What an interesting concept? Charter schools view parents and students as clients. Wow! This is refreshing. This is a huge issue with urban schools. These schools view urban parents not as parents and definitely not as clients, but as unresolved problem. Furthermore, urban teachers lack the type of commitment needed to withstand the difficulties that undoubtedly come with teaching urban students. However, why this insistence or belief system that a new school with a new model is needed to address education plight in urban schools. It seems to me that we have decided that we as a country will continue to limit options when it comes to education and minorities in this country.

The sad reality is, urban students devalue education, and

significantly under-estimate its importance. Often, it's only after they have lived as an adult for quite some time and generate an idea that if I am to acquire a better job, better pay, purchase a home, save for retirement, help invest in my kid's education—I need an education first. If you conduct research about urban students going back to school later, you are likely to find no data. However, this fact does not weaken my argument. According to the National Center for Education Statistics, in 2009, students aged 25 an older accounted for roughly 40 percent of all college and graduate students [thus] experts speculate that this phenomenon has occurred because a significant number of retirees find themselves out of the workforce earlier than they expected, and other students go back to school to acquire new skill sets to launch a second career or move in a slightly different direction.[13] I am not hesitant to accept that data as accurate because these are all legitimate reasons why older Americans go back to school years later. But ex-urban students also find themselves going back to school years later as I suggested earlier. That said, it just goes to show that the impact urban schools have on urban life and ex-urban students reaches and effects black and brown communities in this country. Although this is true, many ex-urban students, now urban parents fail to acquire the education they desperately desire and often need. It becomes an uphill battle and constant rollercoaster to balance school with the demands of life. As a result, urban parents become byproducts and statistics of urban schools.

On a typical day, urban students wonder urban streets and ravaged communities searching for signs of life, but what they find are signs of unyielding and uncontrollable despair. Dilapidated houses and buildings, half-gated projects with little or no grass, the handicap riding electric wheelchairs in the street because of limited sidewalks, young teens walking around with their pants to their knees, young girls either pregnant or barely clothed as early as twelve years of age, stop signs sprayed with graffiti indicating a gang territory, basketball rims net-less, parks that resemble a tornado just swoop in through the night, crack heads on every corner, and prostitutes looking for work.

But what this marks is a group of innocent persons victimized by urban school education. These deplorable conditions and images urban students witness, reduces the likelihood of success by urban schools. Urban schools are conscious of this social construct that threatens their progress but fail to take the necessary precautions to protect urban students against these known variables.

Urban communities are filled with untapped and unused potential, yet, even worse, unrealized potential. Urban schools are not just ruining lives, but worse, destroying them. Individuals, communities, and all sorts of institutions have an obligation to understand why the pushout of [urban students]—the collection of policies, practices, and consciousness that fosters their invisibility, marginalizes their pain and opportunities, and facilitates their criminalization—goes unchallenged.[14] They are sending ex-urban students to their grave void of an opportunity to succeed in life. Every day, some innocent, unsuspecting, uninspired urban youth is victimized by urban schools and its insistence to jeopardize a student's life by not giving a dam what his or her future could look like or be. Urban schools, teachers, and parents enter into a mutual contract where schools solemnly swear and promise to educate the urban student adequately and fairly. Even if there is no written contract that articulates this as such; verbal contracts are also legally binding. Urban schools continue to breach this contract and as I mentioned earlier, state governments and boards of education are complicit in this sham. Monique phrases it this way. She writes, "as institutions with a mission to educate children, public schools are overtly shaping the minds of future leaders, architects of opportunity, and civilians of all types."[15] Princeton Professor John Dilulio Jr. puts it this way.

He writes in part. Not that we can't understand where they come from ... [Think] about how many inner-city black children are without parents, relatives, neighbors, teachers, coaches, or clergymen to teach them right from wrong, give them loving and consistent discipline, show them the moral and material value of hard work and study, and bring them to cherish the self-respect that comes only from respect for the life, liberty and property of others. Think how many black children grow up where parents neglect and abuse them, where other adults and teenagers harass and harm them, where drug dealers exploit them. Not surprisingly, in return for the favor, some of these children kill, rape, maim, and steal without remorse."[16]

First, I must say, I take significant offense to this last statement made by the professor and disagree with some other claims or assertions. But he is spot on when he talks about the neglect of our urban students and someone to teach them from right and wrong, and the importance of valuing hard work and studying. This is a constitutional crisis and urban schools are willfully and intentionally clashing with the 14th amendment to the U.S. Constitution. I cannot be any clearer while making this claim. We must accept things as they are presented, and the evidence overwhelmingly supports my contention. It is time out for sugar-coating the truth. Governments can scream school choice until their tonsils turn blue; urban schools can be fixed, but there lacks legitimate political will because it will threaten private prisons and capitalism.

Chapter 5
Beyond Race, Segregation, Desegregation and Re-segregation

Just over 50 years ago, the Brown decision determined that segregated schools were inherently unequal and began to pave the way for desegregation in other sectors of society. In Gratz v. Bollinger, the Court decided that the University of Michigan's use of racial preferences in undergraduate admissions did "violate the Fourteenth Amendment." Although the Court again recognized the state's compelling interest in achieving student body diversity in higher education, an undergraduate admission policy that automatically awarded every underrepresented minority applicant 20 points was not sufficiently narrow and did not meet the necessary standard that each applicant receives individualized review."[17]

One of the Court's most notable rulings in the area of primary and secondary education was its 1971 decision in *Swann v. Charlotte-Mecklenburg Board of Education*. The *Swann* decision considered a variety of remedies, including the use of racial "quotas' and mandatory school busing, to achieve integration in North Carolina's Charlotte-Mecklenburg area school system. The case involved a school district that had been subject to a state-imposed (de jure) system of segregation and was under a court-supervised plan to desegregate the district. A unanimous Court clarified that "the objective today remains to eliminate from public school all vestiges of state-imposed segregation." It upheld the power of courts to employ a wide range of strategies to achieve that objective, including policies that used a prescribed ratio of white to black students as a legitimate starting point to achieve integration of a segregated district.[18]

In his book *Unfinished Business: Racial Equality in American History*, Michael J. Klarman maintains that housing segregation has increased over the past 50 years, and because most students attend neighborhood schools, housing segregation inevitably means school segregation."[19] Segregation in today's schools arises from such spatial segregation. Re-segregation has not gone unnoted by local school boards. Many local boards have sought to craft school admission policies that take spatial segregation into account to mitigate the effect of neighborhood school assignments on school demographics and to achieve diverse, racially integrated primary and secondary public schools.[20] Klarman's basic point is that law has played an ambiguous role in the history of American racial equality."[21] He further argues that racial progress has resulted more from advocacy and other developments, and that progress itself has been episodic, moving backwards as often forward.[22] Klarman contends that "*Brown* desegregated few public schools before 1964, but ... it nonetheless played a critical role in racial transformation."[23]

The practical hope and less realistic belief were that *Brown* would equal the playing field for minority students in public education because white's dollars would have to remain or travel with them. As a result, black students would be the benefactor of those dollars. I would be kidding if I didn't keep it real and admit, yes that makes sense. How and where dollars are allocated from is a complex scheme. The federal government is usually the source of only about 10 percent of local education dollars. The most well-known source of federal education dollars is Title I of the No Child Left Behind/Elementary and Secondary Education Act, which is mostly allocated to schools and districts with high percentages of poor children.[24] States typically provide about 50 percent of local education funds. Each state has its own system for distributing these funds to school district, and the formulas can be very complex. In Washington State, for example, everything from school enrollment to staff experience level is used to figure out how much money each school district receives each year.[25] A recent study conducted by the U.S. Department of Education indicated that high school seniors in Mississippi received a staggering estimate of $33,000 less in state funding compared to the national average over the course of their public education in a 12 year period.[26] That said, we know that Mississippi is one of the, if not the poorest state in the union thus, money is scarce when tax dollars must be spent on infrastructure, education, and public safety.

This chapter is intended to push back against those that believe that well-balanced integrated schools will fix our broken urban schools and throwing more money at the problem will reconcile urban school's problems. This assertion alone is a cop-out and an excuse used by urban schools to continue down their destructive paths of failing urban students. The solid goal and purpose behind integrated schools is to ensure minority students can benefit from good teachers and a robust curriculum. News flash—the reason why urban schools struggle to attract good teachers and develop robust curriculum is because the culture in those schools are corrupt. The culture is corrupt because too many urban students devalue and take for granted education. What is worse—is these schools overwhelmingly understands this problem but choose not to fix it. It's important to remember that some really good things and students come out of urban schools but overshadowed by its immense and significant problems.

As part of my research, I am not only a product of urban schools, taught in urban schools, continue to mentor in urban school and communities—I also have visited tons of charter schools that have enrolled the same urban students from urban schools that have managed to fail miserably in educating urban students. I ask you to seriously ponder what's the difference between urban students and urban schools and suburban students and suburban schools? We know on the surface each student no matter where she is from or school she attends, has the ability to learn. But, too often in urban schools the best and brightest are not able to engage the learning process for growth. Also, the students that desire more attention are not able to receive the academic attention required. I may sound like a broken record, but I will continue to say this repeatedly, urban schools need to develop a serious academic culture that refuses to give up, quit, and permit urban students to break away from this concept. If the students fail to get it, the schools will continue to fail to implement this concept. The students must row the paddles in order for the boat to go. It is just that simple. Without willing participants, which in this case—are students, the proper academic culture will never come into existence.

It was a Monday afternoon around lunch time. I entered the grounds of this charter school I had heard so much about. I got out of my car and headed towards the front entrance. Before I could get there, I noticed students in a single line heading to lunch without any adult supervision. The stunning part was these students were quietly making their way to lunch. WOW! I thought this could not be the same group of kids that attended an urban school. This wasn't like private school because kids are giving more freedom and encouraged to explore their creative and intellectual voices. The scene resembled a prison line I imagined. I spoke and many of them respectfully responded with a proper greeting. I entered the building and immediately noticed college flags posted throughout on every inch of the wall. I immediately understood what the school was doing. It was simple. Many of these students had never thought about the prospect of attending college. Many of them would be considered first generational college students. Many of them had no one to seek for college advice. The school deliberately had chosen to build an expectation around education after high school.

"Good morning," I spoke.

"Good morning, you must be Mr. McCullough."

"Yes, I am and it's a pleasure to meet you."

"Before she could say anything else, I immediately told her how impressed I was with what I had seen so far."

She replied, "thanks."

"You are welcome."

"Eagerly, I asked. "How did you get the kids to become so well-behaved?"

"Well it definitely wasn't easy or as hard as people think. Two things we know. Students respond differently with expectations and love. So, we knew that reshaping their minds around the education process was critical. But we also knew that we had to hire the right staff to accomplish both goals. We seriously vet our teachers. One thing we learned through vetting was that teachers who graduated from urban schools and lived in urban communities could relate more effectively to students and their parents. We noticed that many of these teachers were sincere about helping urban students achieve because they understand many of their issues faced outside of the classroom. However, if a teacher cares and wants to make a difference, she will be successful. We also knew that it had to be an approach that just didn't involve the kids but their parents as well. We were determined to get parents to buy into this process alone with their kids. The goal was to help the parents feel comfortable and to let them know we were on their side and wanted to help them in any way possible. In order to accomplish this, we host college fairs and job fairs for parents and we regularly hold family night to show parents how to get involve in their student's education."

"WOW."

"All of this totally makes since. I have been arguing this for years even before I had any experience as a teacher or mentor with urban students. It just made sense to me and you and so many other charter schools have proven this."

"You are free to walk around the campus and walk into classes to see what the culture is like."

"Thanks, that would be great."

"Class after class, I noticed engaged instructors and just as engaged students."

I reported back to the principal office to reveal what I had seen.

"Would you like to speak to some of the kids one on one for your research?"

"That would be more than awesome and helpful."

The young man walked into the room where I sat.

"My name is Jamal and I am one of the founding students of ReImagine Prep."

"Nice to meet you."

"Can I ask you some questions?"

"Sure."

"What was the most difficult part of your transition from your past school to this school?"

"I think the hardest part was all the rules and excessive school and homework, but I got used to it."

"What would you say is the primary difference between your old school and this school?

He responded eagerly, "Oh, that is easy. The teachers at my old school seem not to care. They would text often in the classroom, and I noticed many of them wanted to be our friends instead of our teacher. Now that I'm here, I understand my old teachers didn't have my best interest at heart or have any expectations for me."

"Wow," I responded

I thanked Jamal for his candid, intelligent responses and wished him tons of success in his future endeavors.

I spoke to several other students. The responses were similar. An overarching theme I heard was love and expectations. Many of these students for the first time were experiencing love and expectations.

So, I asked, "why do you academically perform differently here opposed to your old school."

Eagerly, they replied, "because the teachers here care and want me to succeed." Most of them admitted not having college aspirations before attending Reimagine Prep. I was not shocked at any of the responses. But my heart could only sob even more because these students were lucky.

The other students in urban schools were not as lucky. But I am convinced that this problem is manufactured and all the money and integration possible will not solve this problem without restructuring and reshaping the culture that exist in urban schools.

Chapter 6
Make America Great Again

"We have to be willing to wish for every other group what we wish for our own if we are to make the identification of the public good our group work. The public good is hampered when we idolize our slice of the social welfare and elevate our group above all others in the political order. Such a thing is bad enough if groups simply aspire to unjust social dominance, but if they've got the power to get it done, it greatly harms the commonwealth."[27]

President Trump's veil reference to "make America great again" deserves my attention. Many thoughts come to mind as I think about Trump's insistence and persistence to use such rhetoric. What America could he be referring to I often think? Although this country is far from perfect, one thing is certain—many nations seek to emulate the United States, and many foreigners leave their country to seek freedom, democracy and the capitalistic opportunities that comes with it. This is the greatest country in the world despite its flaws. This country's history is imperfect but its insistence to right its wrong is the story that prevails. This is the America I am proud to know, and although it is not perfect; its willingness to progress to reach social order and fairness, establishes America as already great.

Seriously, you know what drives me up the wall? This implicit message behind Trump's message that signals somehow America was only great when it was predominantly white. I am aware that you did not expect to read this in a book that makes an assertion that urban schools are assaulting the 14th amendment, but if you are patient, I believe I can connect Trump's "Make America Great Again" slogan to the poor state of education in urban schools.

If Trump would say, let's make America better, or America is better than this, or Americans deserve better than what its government is doing, I would agree. America must do better, particularly, with its urban schools. President Obama spoke to the graduating class of 2016 from Howard University. He stated in his inaugural address, "I remarked that just 60 years earlier, my father might not have been served in a D.C. restaurant—at least not certain of them. There were no black CEOs of Fortune 500 companies. Very few black judges.... We're no longer only entertainers, we're producers, studio executives. No longer small business owner—we're CEOs, we're mayors, representatives, Presidents of the United States."[28] That last fact, I can imagine the students shouted with excitement, tears hanging off eye-lids, mixed with internal subtle disbelief.

There's no doubt blacks have and continue to experience exponential achievement and success outside of being entertainers. Here lies the problem. What blacks are experiencing the success Obama so adamantly speaks of with passion. I assure you a majority of the blacks he attaches these accomplishments to did not attend urban schools. Of course, any assertions I make are debatable. I will say this for the last time—success stories absolutely come out of urban schools. Remember, the problem is that not enough success stories are from urban schools. Yes, President Obama was right for highlighting the successes blacks continue to experience, but this muddies the waters for average Americans that are clueless as to how urban schools operate. This is the policy Washington should be concerned with next to foreign policy. Instead, they preach jobs, jobs, jobs, but urban communities are infested with low-skill workers that stem from their urban education. Urban students aren't going to Howard, Yale, Harvard, or Princeton. They resort to community colleges and local schools where they and the professors learn just how far behind urban students are on the educational scale.

America can only reach its true potential when all students regardless of their race, economic status, and where they are educated—receive a quality education. In this country, we talk about poverty and dependency, but truthfully, urban public-schools are designed to push minority students into a vicious cycle of poverty, which they have significant familiarity. How do you defeat the enemy—if it's all you know. Urban students can only begin to defeat the unknown by realizing that acquiring survival kits can be achieved through hard-work—not a handout. Monique Morris has written a beautiful, powerful book entitled *"PushOut: The Criminalization of Black Girls in Schools"* that articulates how young girls are constantly pushed out of the education system. She narrates a story about a young girl that silently questions her first disciplinary experience.

She writes. "I was in the 5th grade, and this boy, he kept spitting them spitballs through a straw at me while we were [sic] taking a test. I told the teacher, and he told him to stop, but of course, he didn't. He kept doing it. So, I got up and I yelled at him, and he punched me in my face, like in my eye … my eye was swollen and everything … I don't even remember if I fought him, cause that's just how it ended, I think. But I remember that we both got suspended. I was, like, a victim … all the girls rushed to my side, they took me down to the nurse and then, it was just a mess."[29]

Monique interprets this young girl's experience as unintentional and perplexing confusion because as she deemed it, her male classmate was wrong, so why was she being punished for his actions. At that moment, she developed a new way of thinking about school protection. She believed she was a victim, but the institution victimized her innocence. "As she understands it, she was likely to face suspension under most circumstances involving conflict, no matter the particular circumstances."[30]

The assumption follows, why should I give a dam about teachers and schools expecting me to behave in a certain manner. It makes sense right. A logical student assumes that if I'm being bullied or mistreated—I should have the right to protect myself. There is certainly nothing wrong with this raging idea because it's completely sound. But the urban public-school tells urban students that no party is innocent or blameless. Think about the hypocrisy. Urban students are taught to obey rules that undoubtedly will carry forward to adulthood, but their obedience is not rewarded. This is called, continuing not "make America great again."

Individuals on the right side of the political aisle believe government programs create dependency. There is some validity to that argument. Those on the left side of the political agenda believe poor people deserve assistance because the capitalism system is unfair, and typically, benefit those with the best education and access to wealth and credit. There also is some undeniable validity to that argument. However, why Washington argues about how much we should give or don't give to poor communities, they fail to hold urban schools accountable for the epic failure of under and mis-educating these students. The logic is simple. You improve the quality of urban school education and a net reduction in government dependency is achieved. However, this simple logic clearly eludes Washington's radar. Maybe because Washington thinks its job is to go there and persist in rhetoric that borders useless banter.

Michelle Rhee, puts it this way, "when it comes to making laws and policies in the best interests of educating our children, our political system is too often stuck, paralyzed, and dysfunctional."[31] This is a sad reality for the students who are trapped in these schools. It is no secret that a less than adequate education equals poverty. Poverty translates to government assistance for poor people. Paradoxically, republicans believe that government assistance creates dependency, but also believe that urban schools should have the autonomy to run their schools as they desire. Imagine that. Give schools independence that somehow have failed to figure out how to adequately educate its students and to hire and retain good teachers. Sure, that makes tons of sense!

I once heard someone say, if you want to keep knowledge from someone, put it in a book. In today's technological and social media driven society, our youth have become more isolated and read books less than ever. This means it is easier than ever to hide information from our youth. This is a disaster for our youth in general, but more devastating for students that attend urban and schools. In many black communities, reading is not valued. If you are black and reading this book, but disagree with my assertion, I welcome a robust, honest, debate. It is no secret, reading ignites imagination and generates ideas. It is no secret that reading develops critical thinking skills, and it is no secret that it improves comprehension and vocabulary. Reading is one of the most important cornerstones to achieving success and realizing the power of capitalism. Heck, I can't remember reading an entire book while in middle or high school. I didn't enjoy it. Reading was a value in my home for a short period—so as it dwindled, an expectation that I must read, died also.

I cannot help but wonder if collusion is a part of this downfall among urban schools. Maybe it is a stretch to jump to such a leap of logic, but what else can explain such outright failure and an inability by urban schools to address fundamental problems in these school systems. The evidence may be circumstantial at best, but certainly the evidence is strong enough to create a credible and substantial argument that collusion exists between the government and urban schools. Certainly, you have heard the word collusion entirely too much between Mueller, Trump, and Washington politicians, but just follow me briefly as I make the case a collusion argument.

Urban schools have consistently failed these students. Each year their school districts receive grades "C" through "F." In Mississippi, the state gauges this grade through a system called the "Mississippi Statewide Accountability System," and it uses a single "A" through "F" school district accountability system based on requirements of Mississippi Code 37-17-6 and the federal Elementary and Secondary Education Act of 1965 (ESEA). The accountability system assigns performance classifications based on: (a) student achievement, (b) student growth, (c)graduation rates, (d) participation rate, and € other outcome measures.[32] In 2016-2017, the Canton Public School District (CPSD) was labeled with a "D." In 2015-2016, the CPSD was labeled an "F." In 2014-2015, the CPSD was labeled a "D." In 2013-2014, the CPSD was labeled a "D." In 2012-2013, the CPSD was labeled a "D."[33] I hope you are detecting a pattern. These low performing grades stem back several years. I rather not highlight every year because I think I have made my point. In Clarksdale Municipal School District (CMSD), the grades are similar. For example, in 2016-2017, CMSD was labeled a "D." In 2015-2016, the CMSD was labeled an "F." In 2014-2015, the CMSD was labeled a "D."[34] In 2016-2017, the Jackson Public School District (JPSD) was labeled an "F." in 2015-2016, JPSD was labeled "F." In 2014-2015, the JPSD was labeled "D." In 2013-2014, the JPSD was labeled a "D."[35] Among the three schools I highlighted, a very important factor exist besides the consistent failing grade. That is, each school district is populated with over 90 percent of minorities.

It is outrageous that these school districts are labeled with the same grade year after year, but somehow fail to improve its education system. After each assessment and review, the same thing occurs. Several meetings occur within school districts how to better and best educate urban students. Excuse me, but I refuse to believe that these individuals have failed to realize how to best educate students. This leads me to the collusion argument. Collusion must be intentional. I am afraid to suggest that individuals are conspiring how to best fail urban students, but this argument is plausible for many I would argue, including myself.

The dramatic and alarming insistence to reframe from taking a holistic approach to educating urban school students is mind boggling. This is not an outright indictment against teachers and administrators because I highly presume that state government plays an immense role in this sad state of public affairs. But I also think teachers and administrators have an obvious responsibility to not close their eyes to what seems to be collusion, unless you are a part of the unresolved problems that exist in these schools. Otherwise, you should be inside state capitols advocating and arguing for the type of independence needed to adequately educate urban school students.

Some will say that it is absurd to think that the government intentionally has sought to jeopardize urban school student's opportunity to achieve success. Is it really? Jails are filled to the capacity and when jail enrollment decreases, laws tightened. We know that to reduce recidivism, we need policies and programs that will aid the ex-prisoner to make a transition back into society. That means we need laws on the book that encourages employers to give ex-inmates employment regardless of the offense committed. We need programs that help train the ex-inmate so that he can make a smoother transition into society. I would even provide ex-inmates with temporary housing and financial assistance. Why not? We have single mothers on government payrolls that sometimes never come off.

Black students are often labeled lazy and detached from the fruits of educational attainment. Blacks in general are also labeled as angry and fail to take responsibility for their own misfortune. Obama believes that black anger keeps people from rising to defeat their conditions, and to realize that they contribute to some of their own conditions.[36] In barbershop, beauty salons, hotel bars, and other settings, blacks that have rose from the depths of unfair and white institutional privilege sympathize with Obama, but it isn't as easy as Obama think it is. Especially, seeing as though Obama is an interracial male in America that can choose to partake in either sets of privilege.

Some have said that black privilege does exist. I have wrapped my mind around this argument to investigate this window of black privilege. If this idea of black privilege does exist, it certainly is not to the degree of white privilege. Maybe they are referring to the admission policies by college and universities that use race as one of the factors. Or maybe they are referring to federal government contracts that require white companies to hire a certain percentage of minorities before bidding and granted a contract. Or maybe they are referring to some blacks being able to live in suburban communities. Or maybe they are referring to black students attending private schools free because he can run a ball. This doesn't sound like black privilege to me. It's seems to me that certain institutions are seeking to even the playing field for minorities, seeing as though historically blacks were disenfranchised from many social, political and economic opportunities.

However, our urban school students are under the misperception and impression that black privilege is parallel to white privilege. Of course, urban schools have not explicitly expressed this idea, but their half-hearted approach and persistent neglect to adequately educate urban students speak to this assumption. Because urban schools are failing to address this issue, urban students graduate from urban schools to only realize the world is much different than it looks from inside urban school's corridors that depict institutional hypocrisy. Hypocrisy in the sense that school leaders claim to espouse moral and ethical standards but are permitting urban students to espouse the opposite values that are critical to survival in what many still call white American. White America in a qualitative sense, not quantitative. Michael Eric Dyson takes on this "black anger" assertion by Obama.

Dyson writes in part. Obama fails to point out to working-class and middle-class whites who feel that they have worked hard for what they got, and that they do not benefit from their whiteness, that blacks and other minorities feel the same way but with a twist they too worked hard, built from scratch, saw their jobs sent overseas, had their pensions cut, suffered depressed wages, and endured deferred dreams, but got denied the advantages that even white immigrants could take for granted. In short… black folk have endured everything that white immigrants have endured, except they worked in chains and under the fateful wings of Jim Crow. Unlike immigrants that got the benefit of their whiteness to work from scratch and earn their way into the American mainstream.[37]

Interesting, urban school students have no clear sense of the historical misfortunes of blacks. Misfortune may be a very generous word to describe black's conditions surrounding segregation and Jim Crow, but my point remains, urban school students have no true sense of the ravaged and unfair conditions their ancestors endured. However, do we blame these students, of course not. We blame these schools for allowing these students to live in a bubble that does not educate them about the horrors of slavery and segregation. Sure, we may be a covert post-racial society, but that isn't good enough to let urban students to sit on the back of the bus. No, we must teach these kids to take bold stances, a stance like Rosa Parks did on that day to deny a white man her sit because she believed it was time for racial equality.

Maybe some political ideologues on the right are thinking that African American history that focuses on blacks cruel, unwanted, and inhumane treatment is a topic that won't benefit urban school students. Maybe you are right. I am not certain. All I know is that urban schools must use all their resources to motivate and inspire these students to embrace education. We must find a way to prick urban school student's conscience about the necessary moral compass required to forge a better tomorrow. I know we all agree regardless of our politics that our kids are the future. We look to them for a better tomorrow, but if we are only looking to "Make America Great Again" for one race of people, how does this really help this nation's democratic ideals last.

Maybe you are saying, I didn't expect to read about segregation and discrimination in a book that addresses urban school's problems. But remember, urban schools are concentrated with largely black students. And you must understand that these students are being deceived as though we live in a true post-racial society. They are being duped to believing the game is fair for all regardless of your race. As a parent of three black boys, I continue to tell them about black racial disparities. I continue to admonish the importance of valuing education and the hard work that must follow. I continue to tell them that you have no choice but to do these things, and it hinges on your ability to be considered for that position that a white man will be considered for because of the color of his skin. Maybe some of you may think my politics on race have no place in the urban school context. But tell that to Michael Brown and Travon Martin who were essentially kill because of the color of their skin. These are real conversations necessary to sustain the black race in this country, and to take an oblivious position is to do so at the peril of the black race.

Urban schools need to be held accountable for their misdeeds. Pushing these students out unarmed with not only an education that will help them to compete for jobs in the 21st century, but to push them out without a clue about the social injustices that they undoubtedly will face. He is in double jeopardy. Urban school students will surely face situations that reflect social injustice in this country. The question is never if, but when.

We were good friends. We both attended urban schools. We realized that the system had cheated us a great deal. Many of our conversations surrounded this topic. To graduate was one thing but to be prepared for post-secondary education was something different. We were each other support systems outside of immediate family. Something had changed after one year of college. We knew in order to survive the demands of a four-year education, we had to work harder. Our peers seemed to grasp the information effortlessly, but we struggled to learn many of the concepts that were refreshers for them. What a travesty of the American urban education system I thought. We would talk for a couple hours some nights about the horrors of being called on and not wanting to be figured out. What could I be referring to? We didn't want other students to know that we had no clue what the professor was talking about. I can remember days when the professor would lecture, and all I thought "oh my God, I don't have an idea what he is teaching." This was routine and common for about three years. The pain of not knowing and academically struggling haunted both of us.

At the end of the semester, I was placed on academic probation. I had no real interest in pursuing my academic potential any longer—besides my grades reflected a resounding lack of potential. But deep down inside, I desired to challenge my academic capacity. I had never stretched my brain before, so I thought, just maybe I had what it would take. That next semester I attended school with an unwavering commitment and discipline to undo what urban public education had done to me. I could hear my counselor telling my mother, "he isn't college material, why not encourage him to take up a trade." Those words and the reality of being duped by urban education transformed my thought process, and I adopted a relentless approach to education. Dyson writes, "I suppose, in retrospect, it would be fair to say that one of the reasons I became an intellectual was to talk back to suffering—and if possible, to relieve it. I wanted to be as smart as I could be about the pain and heartache of people, I knew were unjustly oppressed.

In retrospect, I believe that I fought and continue to fight as hard as I do to relieve all the pain and suffering, I've endured over the years. Being fired from every job, being told you are not a good fit, being told have you ever thought about working in sales or being indefinitely suspended from an urban school district because I wanted the students to recognize their potential. I was the oppressed that Dyson speaks of, but I know others need to hear my story. That's why I continue to rise to defeat the odds. I inspire urban students daily how not to become a victim of the system, but to be a part of the solution as I.

This is what makes America great. See, America is great but to maintain that greatness, urban students must be adequately educated. I am a product of this system, so I speak truth to power when I express certain criticisms that others choose not to engage. I want to save as many urban students as possible, but one man cannot fight this battle alone. It will take like-minded, passionate advocates for fair, competitive urban school education. And it will take individuals like me who rose up from urban schools to achieve success to reach back and pull as many urban students out as possible.

Chapter 7
Education is Democracy

"Kids are resilient, and those that are on the college track are going to stay on the college track. It's the average kids that are going to suffer because of a lack of funding. Public education remains one of the nation's most ripe environments for inequality. ...According to Jennifer, a special education student who was never able to fully develop her relationship with schools, educators and other key stakeholders have to take a more pro-active role in explaining to girls why education is so important to their development. Make them care more about their education, she said. Cause a lot of these [urban students] don't think education is important..."[38]

The pursuit for equity in education is one thing as I see it—but academic enlightenment is something different. What does it mean to be enlightened? Enlightenment means to develop a new awareness or to see something differently than you had not seen it before. The urban student that is never enlightened by the potency and power that lies in education, will fail to experience true happiness that comes with the freedoms of democracy. Urban students are not physically bound but are mentally and psychologically confined to restrictive and restrained thinking that obstructs their hidden potentials.

For years, education has been viewed as the principle equalizer to equality for all. In Frederick Douglass' narrative, he powerfully writes, "To the slave owner, the prospect of an educated slave was a dangerous notion since he would be more unmanageable than those without learning."[39] This idea of an educated populist is popular, but during the time of slavery, it was frightening for slave owners. In Douglass narrative, he believes that in order to restrict slave owners from educating their slaves, it required punishment by law. For example, in North Carolina, law makers put into place mandates that made it a crime for slave owners to teach their slaves how to read.[40] Largely, these laws were put into place because slave-drivers understood in order to continually oppress blacks, ultimately, blacks had to remain a subjugated people without hope; instead dwell in despair.

I articulate Frederick Douglass' words to set the stage on democracy, and how democracy was not afforded to all races. The only way blacks are able to enjoy democracy is through achieving educational equality. But alone the way, minority students have gotten away from this principal concept, and education stakeholders continue to simply not address the problems in predominantly urban school districts. Dewey believed that a concentrated emphasis was necessary for the transmission of education, and failure would precipitate a civilized group into "barbarism and then into savagery."[41]

One cannot be certain if Dewey is being truly literal about his "barbarism and savagery" argument. But the idea is at least worth considering or debating. Let us think about what barbarism and savagery really means. Both terms allude to a state or condition of being unlearned, uncivilized, and essentially, inferior to others. Maybe a suggestion that urban school students are uncivilized stretches the point. But the point I am attempting to make is that these students at best, lack a cosmopolitan pedigree. It is not to say that they cannot learn. But it is to point out that critical stakeholders fail to do what Dewey suggest. That is, it is obvious that teaching and learning is a necessity for the continued existence of a society.

In a perfect world, utopia would exist in urban schools. Utopia is not a bad idea in an education setting, but too impractical. To educate requires specific and deliberate intent. The goal must be the evolution of an individual or society collectively. What are we talking about here, really? Are we talking about arming these students with knowledge or power that transcends mental understanding? Yes, knowledge is a tool that empowers, but many have it, but fail to attract and gravitate to the right laws of nature. In fact, I would argue that the goal is to get these students to realize the awesome opportunity and responsibility that comes alone with not just knowledge, but also influence. The power to cure homelessness, poverty, incurable diseases, and to develop the next piece of technology that can change the way we communicate, transport goods, or have surgery on a patient. These are the things that stem from knowledge and power. Because knowledge is power, knowledge must be used for good, not tyranny. Case and point, the United States have nuclear weapons to protect this nation and to deter bad actors from thinking about nuclearizing this country. These students deserve the same opportunities as other kids with even more resources.

Dewey writes about the nature and meaning of environment:

We have seen that a community or social group sustains itself through continuous self-renewal, and that this renewal takes place by means of the educational growth of the immature [students] of the group. By various agencies, unintentional and designed, a society transforms uninitiated and seemingly alien beings into robust trustees of its own resources and ideals. Education is thus a fostering, a nurturing, and a cultivating process.

Dewey's analysis is spot on. In fact, I believe the immature and imprudent students that we speak of, lack the discipline of educational rigor. The rigor is necessary to help urban students rise beyond their current state or condition. A renewal of the mind and conscience must align with each other so the urban student can embrace this new challenge. The process will be a difficult one, unimagined by any sense of the imagination, but required. If he is to challenge his old way of thinking or perceived way of living, this process is of practical necessity that transcends symbolism. He cannot reach this point alone. School culture is a critical aspect to help him reach this phase. Teachers must adopt this approach to ensure the student adopts this framework. He can only achieve this new way of thinking and living, it will require diligent dedication. Teachers must help the students recognize and understand the process is larger than he. The student must espouse a set of principles that drives his unwavering commitment, and I would argue faith to see his way through the muddy clouds of uncertainty. He must take on a new identity. He must release himself from a subjugated thought process. His desire to academically succeed must be relentless because he desires to capture the nucleus of democracy. He must learn to lead, not follow. He must learn to be inspired. His willingness to conquer this new attitude on academic life must take on a surreal form that surpasses his own understanding and present reality. He must begin to speak, live, and breathe as a provocative intellectual. He must learn to question the world he lives and has become accustomed. He must be exposed to a different way of thinking and living. His support systems must even find ways to take him outside of his normal environment to keep him motivated. If you ask me, neither of these requirements sound easily achievable, nor will it be easily obtained.

Education has been seen equal in some respects by some so long as students are provided with adequate school resources. Hence, the playing field is assumed level, and no excuse should exist. However, many data depict that students in overwhelmingly less diverse, but predominately minority school districts have struggled to acquire an adequate college-ready education.

I begin with the premise that no one would ever tell their child to drop out of school, infers that achieving an education is fundamental to student's desired success. This conversation must not center around acquiring a document that articulates very specific words, that presumably implies that a student is either college or career ready. The presumption itself is too presumptuous and requires more narrative. In fact, the middle and high school a student attends, often defines his future success.

Education is Democracy

The idea of democracy is the underlying linchpin to success achieved. Democracy is a vast and individual realized concept. But, at its root, democracy is represented by a government institution, by the people, for the people. This is achieved by the people electing government officials to work in government to develop and shape social, political, economic and education policy that represents the ideas of the people. As simple as this may sound, often government leaders are thrust into office, and fail to design and implement the type of policies that are necessary to fix contemporary demanding social issues. In the *"Great Debate: Edmund Burke, Thomas Paine and the Birth of Right and Left,"* Yuval Levin earnestly focuses on analyzing the profound, political, philosophical minds of Burke and Paine.

He writes that for Paine, the natural equality of all human beings translates to complete political equality of all human beings to complete political equality and therefore to a right to self-determination. The formation of society was itself a choice made by free individuals, so the natural rights that people bring with them into society are rights to do as one chooses, free of coercion. Each person should have the right to do as he chooses unless his choices interfere with the equal rights and freedoms of others. And when that happens—when society as a whole must act through its government to restrict the freedom of some of its members—government can only act in accordance with the wishes of the majority, aggregated through a political process. Politics, in this view, is fundamentally an arena for the exercise of choice, and our only real political obligations are to respect the freedoms and choices of others.[42]

Paine is exactly right. People should have the free will and reign to do as one chooses. He is also right that free will and liberty to explore and take advantage of democracy should only be interfered with when he chooses to go beyond the boundaries of true liberty—when he decides that his liberty is more important than his neighbor's liberty, thereby restricting or restraining his neighbor's freedom to explore and take advantage of that same liberty. He is right—only then must society act as a whole through government to produce order. But what happens when urban school students have no idea about what democracy looks like, or what aspects of everyday life are open to democracy.

The urban student's perspective on life blinds his ability to explore and take advantage of the majestic concepts of life, liberty and property. What does he do—when he has been symbolically shackled to a culture and a set of rules that are not the norm outside of urban communities and schools? In 1920, Democrat Senator Pat Harrison, spoke during a hearing and fiercely concluded that a public-school crisis existed n D.C.[43] Fast forward to the 21st century and the issues that plagued D.C. public schools are still at lurk. A group of reporters asked Michelle Rhee, then Chancellor of D.C. public schools an unthinkable question—are you going to be able to open schools on time.[44]

A lack of adequate education for poor and minority schools, engenders vast policy concerns and ramifications for communities and its perceived democracy. Jan Hughes and Oi-Kwok have concluded that African American children are "less conforming and more active than are Caucasian children" in education settings, and this recognizable fact could help urban teachers interact more effectively instead of leveling unnecessary criticism. This social construct should foster immediate education policy concerns in the urban school.[45] The term social policy is mentioned in many academic settings and is used to explain or complain about the condition of different policies, including education policy.

What does it mean to be social? Interesting question, don't you think? We can look on-line and find multiple meanings, but at its core, it refers to social relationships that we engage for comfort or companionship. The word social infers that you have a choice to choose your setting, environment, friends, and the interaction that takes place in your group. So, this idea of social policy is complex in a school setting because it presumes that students will align to its culture without any teaching or instruction. Social policy in education dictates that students must come to school and act a certain way, respond a certain way, and think a certain way. However, this type of thinking fails to address student's issues at its root.

If we are truly concern with student democracy in education, we must realize students in urban schools harbor many issues that cannot and will not be erased by pretending that such issues do not exist. Many students in stricken impoverish areas, battle serious social inadequacies. Thus, students are foreclosed from choosing and engaging many of the social relationships and environments that are conducive to proactive learning.

Steve Perry, principal of a charter school, who enrolls one-hundred percent minorities and sends one hundred percent of his students to college, believes the culprit for failing inner city schools are teachers' unions. Not teachers, administrators, parents, or communities. Steve Perry also believes that leaders in education have become more concerned with not hurting important stakeholder's feelings like teachers, administrators, and school board members, while failing to blame anyone. Steve Perry also believes, there is no proof that kids that grow up in poverty cannot be educated, or they do not have the ability to learn as students from more affluent areas. He believes that unions are creating rules like, how many days and hours a student should attend a year, and how much teachers should be paid and how they should be evaluated.

Steve Perry's assertions are reached due to his administrative experiences and are warranted in my opinion. To this point, the fact that he believes that one entity is the blame for students' lack of academic success, highlights my point of why educational stakeholders must view this problem holistically. No one stakeholder should be blamed, or not blamed, for the inadequacies of the education received by urban students.

Schools' repeated failure to adequately educate students from urban communities creates a human and national crisis. Moreover, it impedes important human potential and capital, while creating a permanent underclass of citizens. The miseducation and mis-opportunities that our urban students experience are practical variables that must be and can be addressed. In order for all relevant stakeholders to promulgate the necessary work to increase urban student's academic success, there has to be a realization that urban students require different attention. This realization must encompass the impact of social costs that it has on our economy because undereducated urban students.

If education leads to democracy, why are so many urban school districts failing our youth. Education is key so that urban students may be able to reach beyond their current situations that encompasses single family homes, mothers working two to three jobs, drug infested neighborhoods, under-educated parents, pandemic gun violence, drug abuse, and high teenage pregnancy rates. The picture painted is gloomy, but reality in many urban or inner-city communities. This saddens me, of course, but even more sad, are school communities and policy makers that take comfort in shifting blame, while urban students pay the ultimate price; the inability to achieve democracy.

Freedom is the linchpin to democracy, but urban students are subjugated by a system designed to under-educate and miseducate them. I am afraid urban students are being counted out and not judged by their ability to learn good character. Urban students must be taught good character, in order to operate under the necessity of it. Dr. King believed in racial harmony and hoped that individuals would be judged by the content of their character, and not the color of their skin. Wow, if he believed that, and after years' civil rights leaders fighting for equality in education, transportation, housing, and public accommodations in order to use the same rest room or be served a meal at the front door, and not back. Why do we judge urban students by the content of their character, when an adequate education helps build and define a student's good character? We are leaving our students without a serious fighting chance.

If it sounds like I am angry, you predict right. All I know is that the education systems in urban communities are dropping the ball, even worse, the educators, administrators, community leaders, government officials, parents and religious institutions are also failing our students miserably. We can hold a million town hall meetings or social roundtables, but what required is taking full ownership of "Shared Blame." It is time out for blaming each other, and it is time to sit, communicate, and listen to urban students about their hopes, fears, anxieties and desires for their future. No one ever desires to listen to the person who is being hurt the most, in this case, the urban student. This must change. It is time out for the political pandering and shifting blame about who does what. Urban students are being robbed of their freedom.

What type of future do we seriously desire for urban students is the pressing and necessary question that must be answered? When I decided to write this book, I told myself I would not make it personal, but it is personal because I attended an urban school. No matter how much people discuss what is wrong with students in urban schools, no one seeks to put forth the practical, necessary policies and actions required to save them. If this is not a tragedy, I am not sure what else qualifies. Yearly, too many people die from gun violence, and too many urban students are robbed of an adequate education. In that order, we as a nation should be concerned with gun policy and education policy in urban schools. We are depriving blameless urban students the opportunity to tap into their unhidden or masked potential to achieve the type of democracy that is predicated on attainment of an adequate education.

Chapter 8
From Urban School to Incarceration

"I say to you today, my friends, so even though we face the difficulties of today and tomorrow, I still have a dream. It is a dream deeply rooted in the American dream."

Before the "Black Lives Matter" movement, social and institutional forces struck at the core of this heated contention depending on what side of the political aisle you identified with. Black politicians, civil rights leaders and many clergymen have long fought to ensure black lives were not a mere afterthought. They have fought to keep black issues relevant and pressing to protect blacks from social, political, and economic disruption and interruption. So, the movement isn't particularly new, but what the movement did was create a new resurgence of young activism. The movement helped to re-shed light on these biased and bigot institutional forces that desire to create an uprising or displacement of black progress and black success.

As an urban student, I became a byproduct of urban thinking. I had no idea that criminal forces existed that unfairly and unjustly targeted black males to an egregious, unparallel degree. "Black boys are policed like no one else, not even black men. Police officers persistently target, stop, and harass black boys wherever they are—on the street, in school, in stores—and no matter what they are doing. Henning explains how police officers see black boys not as children, but as dangerous criminals, even when they are not engaging in criminal or even suspicion behavior."[46] Just maybe there should be a program in urban schools that highlight the statistics surrounding black males and incarceration or at least touch on issues that plague young black males, and the most common ways black males are arrested repeatedly. Maybe my assertion is subjective, but I believe this is objective by many measures.

All that said, if you desired to fit in or be liked by your peers, cool was the rule at my high school. Like every public school, there are clicks. But at my school, I think virtually everyone was cool to varying degrees. I remember I was in the eleventh grade, and I skipped first period to stand in Footlocker's line to purchase the latest pair of Jordans. At my school, to wear Jordans hours after they had come out, symbolized that you were one of the popular kids. This was just one way to be considered cool.

What is my point? I was not hanging out at the bookstore or library working on projects, reading the latest novel, or working on college essays or applications. In fact, although my family insisted that I attend college after graduation, I was grossly underprepared. In fact, from the time I arrived home from school, I hung with friends till darkness fell. I did not read, study, or do homework. I only focused on what I did not understand was not important. Although, I was not getting in trouble, certainly I was not preparing for what would come after high school. My mother was proactive about education, but she often worked two jobs, so she was less visible and involved. See, this is why so many urban school students are in the prison-to-pipeline system. The opponents will argue that urban schools cannot act as surrogate parents. This is true. It is not my attempt to make excuses for parents. I only want readers to realize that this is reality in urban communities. The fact I have acquired three professional degrees years later is a testament to my mother and aunts that taught me the value of education alone with my insistence to succeed.

It was the night after graduation. Hanging with a group of friends trespassing outside a hotel was my first encounter with law enforcement. The offense did not warrant the egregious encounter I experienced. I was surprised beyond imagination. I had never been in trouble or engaged the law before. That night, my life and understanding of being a black man just hours after graduation—shifted. That moment in time sparked a long-standing battle of constant and consistent episodes with law enforcement.

I had a double-barreled shot gun pointed at my back as I hid in a large leafy bush.

He yelled, "put your goddam hands up and come from behind that bush."

"Yes sir," I responded. I thought to myself, I was only here chasing girls and didn't mean any harm. It didn't matter, it seemed to him. He was ready to make an example out of me.

In a state of shock, I uttered all types of expletives to myself. All I thought, I deserved to go home. Why don't you go and fight some real crime, internally I questioned?

"People of color in the United States, particularly young black men, are burdened with a presumption of guilt and dangerousness. Some version of what happened to me has been experienced by millions of black people because of this racially biased presumption. In too many situations, black people are presumed to be offender's incapable of being victims themselves. As a consequence of this country's historic failure to address effectively its legacy of racial inequality, this presumption of guilt and the racial narrative that creates it has significantly shaped every institution in American society, especially our criminal justice system."[47]

Again, I encountered the law during a routine traffic stop. I drove my college roommate from Tuscaloosa to Birmingham, Alabama. The Birmingham police pulled me over for speeding. Unknow to me, there were drugs in my roommate's duffle bag. He immediately told me after being pulled over.

"Crap," I blurted.

I'm going to jail for a very long time. I'm furious he would do something so stupid. I wasn't the most ethical person, but drugs were never my thing.

The officers asked to search the car. I immediately said yes because I figured it would indicate my innocence, and they would decline the search. That did not happen. They searched the inside and trunk of my car. I was sweating bullets—thinking to myself, "Lord" I don't want to go to jail. The search was unsuccessful, and the white cops didn't find anything. Years later after taking criminal law in law school, I learned that they had no legal right to search my car without probable cause.

That's why they asked for my permission. I could have declined their request because they had no probable cause. Now, I also know that certain areas of the vehicle like the trunk or and other compartments were off-limits without specific probable cause. If you ask me, this is critical information every urban student must know. Unfortunately, driving while black can trigger law enforcement to routinely stop you and urban students must understand this.

For the next several years, I would find myself in legal perils. In 2002, I was charged with rape by a female while completing my annual training with the military as an administrator specialist. This episode, again, almost derailed my life. Thank God for a praying family that supported me morally, spiritually, and financially. I was acquitted a year later. The bad news is I was kicked out of University of Alabama's ROTC program, and lost my opportunity to graduate as a commissioned 2nd Lieutenant. At this point, I was devastated because I couldn't understand why I always found trouble, or it found me. These were perplexing and difficult times. But the perplexities and difficulties were not over.

For the next few years, I would be arrested for unpaid tickets in several towns in Mississippi. Each were cash bonds. Now, I found myself in and out of jail, bothered by my prospects of success, and toying with the idea of suicide as much as possible. These were dark moments I never imagined facing. I wondered why I had been cursed or what did I do to deserve such constant, disproportionate hardship. Believe it or not, many black males end up doing real time because of an abundance of unpaid fines.

Judges are supposed to take into consideration his ability to pay based on his income, unemployment, disability or inability to find work because of an ailing economy, but this never occurs.

The 13th Amendment to the U.S. Constitution states that "Neither slavery nor involuntary servitude, except as a punishment for crime whereof the party shall have been duly convicted, shall exist within the United States, or any place subject to their jurisdiction." There is no need to interpret or explain the language. At its core, it means that no person shall be punished without violation of some crime and subsequent conviction by a trial by jury. No one disagrees that a person shall do the time, if he does the crime. A very universal principle, no denial. But, under what universe do we incriminate blameless students under the presumption that their test scores are truly indicative of their academic potential. Why do urban schools have policies that punish students at incomprehensible ages? Why do urban schools have policies that punish urban students for incidents that are not criminal? Here lies the problem that I have with such a foolish and unwarranted notion.

Some of the most unthinkable and erroneous applications of punitive school punishment in this country have criminalized [urban students] at very early ages. Urban students are arrested for classroom disruptions like throwing tantrums in their school classrooms and yelling and screaming at a teacher. For example, "six-year old Salecia Johnson was arrested in Georgia in 2012 for having a tantrum in her classroom."[48] In 2011, seven-year old Michelle was arrested with her eight-year old brother after they got into a fight on an Ohio school bus.[49] A six-year old Desre'e

Watson was handcuffed and arrested at a Florida school in 2007 for throwing a tantrum in her kindergarten class.[50]

These tragic events certainly should not happen in the U.S., but they are. The logic behind these types of arrests are illogical and have no basis. What's the argument for these wildly, absurd arrests of such young students that committed no criminal acts? "While a black prisoner was a rarity during the slavery era—the solution to the black population had become criminalization.... The explicit use of race to codify different kinds of offenses and punishments was challenged as unconstitutional, and criminal statutes were modified with language that contained no explicit racial references, but the enforcement of the law didn't change [thus] black people were targeted for wide ranging offenses that whites were not." [51] Today, this fact remains to ring loudly. However, urban students are the new target of victimization and criminalization. Spending time in prison has become almost an inevitable part of the life cycle for black boys growing up in urban communities. The criminal justice system broadly has come to be viewed by many not as an institution designed to advance public safety but as an oppressive bureaucracy that has implemented a twenty first century version of free labor.

Police commonly and repeatedly set up roadblocks to entrap the urban student or the recent urban student. While miles down the street, a suburban community rarely sees a roadblock where similar criminal behavior exist. The Chicago Tribune reported that Jefferson Park, where one fifth of police officers reside and are predominantly white—bolsters one of the highest rates of drunk driving incidents and fatalities but has failed to set up a sobriety checkpoint there in five years. The report was released in 2015. Seven miles down the street which includes the city's west side of town—those same police have set up numerous sobriety checkpoints. That side of town is predominantly minority and has experienced four-times fewer alcohol related incidents.[52] As a once urban student and urban community resident, I am able to speak truth to these uncanny incidents. Now, as an educated black man that rose from the depths of mis and under-education, I live and socialize in suburban circles. My experiences are vast and credible to the obvious differences how people of color are policed based on where they live, or school attended. I cannot pinpoint or estimate the number of times I encountered a roadblock while living in an urban community. I often said to myself, "I know these dam police have something to do other than harass black people."

I got tired of seeing it because I never saw it done in white communities. It was obvious. In urban communities, a significant number of residents would undoubtedly either have old speeding fines, riding around without insurance, or some illegal substance in their possession. This meant jail time and if you had a cash bond, the entire amount was due. For many urban students and recent urban students, they would have to serve time to work their fine off. Law enforcement knows this act and use these tactics to subject the urban student or recent urban student to the conditions of criminalization. The goal is to push him to the point of hopelessness and despair until he feels a sense of betrayal. "More enduring is the mythology of black criminality and the way America's criminal justice system adopts a racialized lens that menaces and victimizes people of color, especially black men.... The presumptive identity of black men as slaves evolved into the presumptive identity of criminal, and we have yet to fully recover from this historical frame."[53]

I for one couldn't understand the system. I constantly thought to myself, "what in the heck did I do or not do to be exploited by the criminal justice system." A reality we must confront is that alarming rates of drugs are used by urban students. Many of these communities are ravaged with drugs and gun violence. On every corner is a packaged store with ex-urban students on the corner. On that corner, ex-urban students aren't passing out education or religious literature—instead they are looking to prey on current urban students to make a sale or pitch. The urban student is exposed to what they perceive as the only way of life. So, the urban student's opportunity to either do or sell drugs is significantly higher. Of course, law enforcement is aware of this fact—and seizes on the moment when the time is right.

Clarence Aaron was a twenty-three-year-old college student from Mobile, Alabama, with no criminal record. This didn't matter because in 1992 he introduced a young black man to a prospective buyer of drugs who was also black. All three black boys were arrested, and Clarence was sentenced to three terms of life imprisonment in federal prison. Twenty years later, President Obama pardoned his sentence, but Clarence was the lucky one.[54] This is the type of situation the urban student is likely to encounter. The innocent urban student who is just joy riding with a group of friends is clueless to the drugs that are in the car. He admits he has no drugs and has never smoked them.

It doesn't matter, law enforcement will interrogate him to a point that he incriminates himself. These tactics are common placed to get young black boys to admit to crimes not committed. He is sentenced to the juvenile justice system—not for committing a crime but for hanging with the wrong crowd. It's difficult for a black kid to convince law enforcement that he is innocent when he is prematurely labeled a criminal.

I was constantly exploited by the system and couldn't seem to exploit the employment system. I experienced this as an educated black man with two degrees. Society preaches post-secondary education after high school, but the system still rails against black men regardless of his IQ and acquired education. Do I believe post-secondary education is important, without a doubt? As I have learned—it's not about what you know, but who you know. However, who you know isn't enough to shape character. Character education teaches young people how to assimilate into a society that requires proactive, progressive, evolutionary growth to the challenges and demands of society and community living.

The school-to-prison pipeline is not an imaginary problem, but worst, it is a tangible, perverse epidemic. Think about the consequences. More devastating is the fact that our often poor and minority youth are caught in the crossfire of politics and capitalism. A film produced by Ava DuVernay entitled *"13th From Slave to Criminal with One Amendment"* explores modern day slavery. The documentary investigates the modern institution and makes the forceful claim that the 13th amendment is the linchpin that fuels incarceration.

Certain data has shown that private prisons are built based on third graders reading level. If you think this sounds absurd, just research it for yourself, rather than take my word. But this is not the worst part. These numbers are gathered based on students in urban school districts. Think about the plausibility. If you want to determine the potential incarceration rate, would you look to suburban and private schools or urban school districts where many data depict low academic success? The answer is simple.

Across the state of Mississippi, "public schools are hindering the success of children and youth by employing harsh, destructive disciplinary practices [that] exclude students from the classroom thereby reducing learning opportunities [that] trap students in a pipeline to prison cycle." In October 2012, the United States Justice Department filed litigation against the city of Meridian, Mississippi, and two state agencies for operating a school-to-prison-pipeline. Think about that for a moment. The complaint alleged that the actors engaged in deliberate practices that routinely and systematically incarcerated students for minor infractions like refusing to follow directions and profanity usage. These facts are startling to say the least but helps to further emphasize my point why education reform requires a holistic approach. All stakeholders must share the blame to reconcile this problem.

Students are the linchpin to building a brighter future, but what students are the question. Such an ideal has not always been a part of our American fabric that the American Dream was available to all regardless of race, creed, ethnicity, or socioeconomic status. The idea that a group of businessmen are sitting around the table at this moment, waging bets against students in low socio-economic environments, is frightening. It is equivalent to waging a bet against a student not reaching her American dream.

Poor students lack of adequate or equal access to education, or similar quality of instruction as their well-off peers "threatens to shatter this new ideal of economic opportunity" while creating a permanent and isolated group of undereducated, under skilled, and under-employed citizens that result in increased welfare dependency, drug use, participation in illegal activities, and perpetual and increased incarceration. Excuse me why I have a conversation with my conscience.

"What does this resemble to you?"

"What do you think? I'll wait."

"Seriously, you have no idea."

"Are you talking about what the 14th amendment to the constitution guarantees?"

"That's it, the man that is writing this book."

Urban students are being deprived of not just the advantages that stem from a fair and equal education—they are being deprived and neglected of the opportunity to pursue unyielding freedom, happiness, and prosperity.

In many urban schools, zero tolerance policies are designed to open students up to the idea of detention as punishment. Urban schools have strategically decided to not create an environment that is conducive to learning. Thus, the student engages a jail like system early, thereby becoming desensitized to the negative effects prison will have on his future. I would further argue that it creates a dependency on an institution that has no positive benefit for the urban students.

In psychology, "desensitization" is defined as the diminished emotional responsiveness to a negative or aversive stimulus after repeated exposure to it. I mentioned desensitization earlier, but I want to discuss something I have cloned as "Academic Desensitization." That is, students have become emotionally non-responsive to the resulting stimulus achieved from academic engagement. To put it into the proper perspective, I did not experience academic stimulus until my freshmen year of college.

Academic stimulus includes a feeling of self-worth, academic freedom, and an eagerness to learn something new repeatedly. You may be wondering if this is possible. Yes, it is. I correlate it to the first moments of being granted the opportunity to drive. The sense of freedom was invigorating, and I was eager to learn everything required to become a licensed driver. I guess you are wondering, why I did not achieve this stimulus in middle or high school. The simple answer is the wrong culture.

Academic culture is a community of beliefs, principles, and practices centered around academic engagement. Sounds simple right, wrong. Academic culture requires a committed group of stakeholders to academic responsibility. Sounds simple right, wrong. The central stakeholders are the principals, teachers, and students. If you are wondering why I did not mention parents, that is because I am only focusing on the school community. I will get to the parent's roles and responsibilities later. It is no secret that urban schools are vastly different and come with its own unique set of challenges. What makes me uniquely qualified to speak on this topic? I attended such schools and taught in them as well. My perspective is uniquely vast based on personal experience.

First, principals and teachers must have a shared vision. Sure, the principal is the organizational leader, but teachers must be the community leader. What do I mean when I say teachers must be community leaders? Teachers are the first point of contact with students; therefore, teachers demonstrate and communicate leadership. In order for this two-tier leadership to be carried out, principals and teachers must actively engage in professional development continuously to discuss a shared vision, shared goals, and what is not working and what is working. The reason for this is because school modeling must constantly seek improvement, even when it believes it has the perfect formula.

The two most important stakeholders must be in alignment. Principals and teachers must lead in this capacity. Any tension or friction threatens this concept. I have had many intimate conversations with friends and colleagues about teachers leading and exhibiting leadership qualities before their students. Students must not only see or recognize leadership; they must feel a teacher leading. For example, while I was in the classroom instructing students, I made sure that I had a competent command on the subject matter being taught. Just as important, I could always answer a question if a student had one.

Exchanging dialogue with my students, I learned that they admire and respect teachers that are knowledgeable. Curious as to why they thought their teacher(s) were not knowledgeable, they would tell me things like "because he or she would always sit at the desk and teach from the manual." I thought this was interesting. Students were clearly conscious of teachers who were not competent or either lazy. Students also informed me that this often induced them to not engage the academic process.

Think about the simplicity, but severity of a teacher's perceived behavior. Students rationalized through their thought process that incompetent teachers deserved less respect and attention; furthermore, a teacher's incompetence induced students to not engage the academic process. Surely, this tells you how powerful and important a teacher's role. In retrospect, without naming teachers, I can remember one teacher that gave me answers to the exam, another teacher that literally did not teach, and another teacher that decided I did not have the necessary potential to go beyond high school.

I ask, what makes teachers seek such an important position that pays a mediocre wage. It seems to me, since many states underpay teachers, they would acquire their joy from knowing they improved a student's life, saved that student's life, or helped a student become the first in his/her family to attend college. If it sounds like I am teacher bashing, I am. But be reminded, there are some terrific teachers out there that passionately engage the instructional process with vigor and refuses to except less.

Teachers deserve more support. Teacher's hands are tied behind their backs because of unnecessary bureaucracy coming from D.C., and the state. They deserve more pay, freedom to teach, and the ability to play a significant role in the academic policy-development process. It has always perplexed me why do we not seek input from our most important stakeholders, the teachers. These men and women are on the battlefield going to war without the best tools and resources, but still strive to perfection to teach student's the necessary curriculum.

Chapter 9
A Public Policy Crisis

The Great Depression of the 1930s gave rise to unprecedented unemployment, drastic cutbacks in production, sixty percent declines in farm and labor income, widespread business and bank failures, devastating home foreclosures, all reacting on each other in an extraordinary downward spiral. But Congress and President Lyndon Johnson responded to this crisis with the New Deal. A host of government programs that would revive the economy, put people back to work, and provide government subsidies.

Likewise, in 2008, the U.S. economy crashed again, This time, due to a failed housing market. This time, President Obama and Congress responded to this crisis. There was consensus, something had to be done. Congress bailed out Wall Street. Congress gave billions to Big Banks and to Big Car Manufacturers. See, government can respond if it needs. But government refuses to apply the same type of response to the education collapse that occurs in urban school districts.

It is no secret that education is a critical public policy issue that demands urgent attention. But many education leaders and politicians are deliberately undermining how important it is to charge vigorously ahead with necessary reforms in this nation's struggling school districts. I am reminded of the infamous movie, the "Titanic."

Most Americans have seen the "Titanic," and remember its draw-dropping plot. The movie depicts a huge sinking ship filled with people, and a frantic captain that knew he was getting ready to make one of the most unthinkable choices any man could face. He had to assign value to human life. Ultimately, he decided that the wealthy women and their children deserved lifeboats first, men, and the poor people last. Think about that. Now think about it in terms of our education system.

Too many poor students are being left behind, but education leaders and policy makers incautiously go about their day, without realistically giving a dam about our most vulnerable students in society. For the last decade, Congress has managed not to pass an infrastructure bill to fix and improve the nation's highways, bridges, tunnel, dams, airports, and railroads. I am sure you are wondering, why I make this point. Simple, just as our infrastructure system has been crumbling, and continues, urban education system finds itself in a very similar condition.

On August 1, 2007, the I-35W Mississippi River Bridge collapsed into the Mississippi River, killing 13, and injuring 145 people. This was one of the busiest bridges in Minnesota, and many citizens depended on this bridge' stability and capacity to safely travel across. But on that unthinkable day, it happened. Our urban schools are the bridge and daily student's ability to graduate from high school, acquire post-secondary education

A Public Policy Crisis

collapses, and successfully integrate into society are not met.

If this is not a public policy crisis, what is? Poor and minority students are robbed of their opportunity to succeed. If you ask me, the question is simple. What type of nation do we want to be known as? We are the richest country in the Nation, but we cannot fix our struggling school districts. I refuse to buy into it. Someone great once said, if there is a problem, it can be solved. Never have bought into the idea of conspiracy theory, but at this juncture, I have been forced.

What else can explain the redundant stupidity? Allow me to apologize for the brash language, but I become enraged with the politics. Politics should not be inserted into doing what is right for students. Education experts know that educating urban students like students from suburban schools do not work, so why do they insist to perpetuate the model? It just seems to me; it is a really big game. Instead of addressing the real problem, they wrap a ban-aid around it, and focus on non-problems.

Even worst, minority personnel that run these school districts, hunker down, and accept the status quo. The status quo is that these students are a lost cause. If the parents do not care, why should I? Emphatically, I have strong distaste for persons that believe parents are the only line of defense to save urban students. Educators and administrators know this is not true. But they spread this myth to engender resistance by teachers that do not see parents as an excuse to educate students.

To view these students as hopeless, is a public policy crisis. A crisis that demands attention. Students require attention, and someone who is willing to invest in their future. Interesting enough, public policy and democracy are part of the same family tree. Without the right education policies to help urban students, they fail to experience what democracy truly looks or feels like. We speak of the American dream and capitalism, but for many of these students, they will experience the American dump.

Poverty is not a privilege or a right. Poverty is not something someone aspires to achieve. In fact, I do not think it is possible to achieve poverty. To achieve anything takes effort and work. To live with minimum means does not take much effort. It is a public policy dilemma for urban students because they are unaware of the roads they inevitably will travel. A road that is filled with constant disappointment. A life of tragic outcomes. Few will experience the success they see on television.

This public policy issue is about more than just capitalism, and urban students not burdening society. It is about the progression of human life. The ability for urban students to have a seat at the table of productivity. It is about them not having to settle, or being told that you are not college material, or you will be a loser like your mother or father. This is a human crisis that requires public policy to address this issue.

I mentioned that poor people don't achieve poverty. Poverty is a serious public policy issue. There seems to be a dichotomy between poverty and poor education, but there is not. There is a clear link between the two. All research points to it. Society tells us that know other vehicle can help members of society earn wealth than education. Twenty-five years ago, experts said an undergraduate degree was enough. Fifteen years ago, you had to earn a masters to compete. Today, you need a professional degree. The required education levels will continue to move. I wonder what is next. All the while, educators and policy experts are disinterested in dealing with struggling school districts.

Interesting, don't you think? It takes more education than ever to compete. And the U.S. Department of Education has said that science and math must be the new focus in order for students to compete with other countries right now. Meanwhile, students in struggling schools have problems with reading, comprehension, and writing. If urban students cannot compete, they end up in poverty. Something many of these students are accustomed to but have a minimum perception of what poverty really encompasses.

So, it seems that the phrase remains true. If you grow up in poverty, you will remain in poverty. This is a tragic, sad truth. Poverty is not fair or equitable, and certainly no one desires to be in poverty. Poverty not only devastates communities and curtails economic development in many urban communities. Poverty also hampers education growth, other words; students' likelihood to obtain an adequate education.

The corrosive effects of poverty are real. Urban students have a better opportunity of being incarcerated, before making it out of poverty. Maybe I am wrong for asserting this. This is only an unfounded theory. But many teachers teach in the same school districts they attended. Many of these teachers, let's face it, are living check to check. Many of them are even working part time jobs. This is an unfortunate reality. But if these teachers are battling with stagnate wages, and barely make ends meet, why should they care about a low-income student being adequately educated. Yes, this is conspiracy theory at its worst, but there may be something to it. To that end, you must think this through for yourself.

As humans, we somehow feel compelled to adore teachers because it takes a special person to discipline and teach young people. But you must remember, in any profession, there are good and bad personnel. There are some teachers that have no business in a classroom. These teachers add no value to a student's life. I have a request. If you are such a teacher, please submit your resignation ASAP! Without digressing any further. A poor education is the root of poverty, and those that grow up in poverty, often times receive a poor education.

Inadequate education equals crime in most instances. Criminal behavior and the burdens of institutionalization become the norms for many urban students. Crime is a serious public policy issue. But the U.S. Department of Education and the state-run education systems are aware of poorly educated students being a burden on society. Not only aware of their burden on society, the system is designed to push many of these students into the prison system.

Just like Walmart provides services, and needs consumers to buy its millions of products, jails have a service, and need them filled. The calculation is simple. It is a game of capitalism. The private prison system complex depends on criminals. Criminals are the linchpin to their success. What better way to achieve this goal? This is a large part why urban students are inadequately educated. This is why urban students are written off before given an opportunity to engage and enjoy the academic process.

A Public Policy Crisis

The more students become disengaged, equals greater revenue for the private prison complex. State governments do not care, and teachers become frustrated with the ridiculous bureaucracy implemented by State Departments of Education. States and the private system complex collude behind closed doors. The collusion includes how to channel more minorities into their jail cells. I read a report that expressed concerned that a Mississippi jail was losing revenue because crime was down.

Crime was down, and it was articulated like a bad thing. Like the world was at its demise. Excuse me, I thought a reduction in crime was good for society at large. I thought the purpose of the criminal system is to help deter criminal behavior. That is the game played. Just like desegregation was bad for whites and their capitalism. Reduced crime is bad for the CEOs running jails around this country.

The real crisis is that governments and private prisons seek to fill them. This is why drug laws are so unfair. Statistics show that minorities are more likely to sell drugs, rather than just smoking it. Drugs are the number one major offense that causes minorities to be incarcerated.

Not sure about you, but I am fed up with the political tirade. The hypocrisy is sickening. The outright education discrimination in urban schools. The persistent conscious but subtle aggressive tactics to divert attention away from giving low-income students an opportunity at success. How is it okay that these institutions are systematically oblivious to the needs of these students? Only one reason. Indifference to their needs. These students need policies that reflect their struggles that are at the root of their problems.

Chapter 10
Time for Due Process

It is speculated that the Founding Fathers wrote and passed the United States Constitution between May and September of 1787.[55] According to Library of Congress, the 14th Amendment to the United States Constitution was ratified July 28, 1868.[56] "The amendment grants citizenship to all persons born or naturalized in the United States, which included former slaves that just had been freed after the Civil War. The amendment had been rejected by most southern states [and] it is known as the Reconstruction amendment that forbids any state to deny any person life, liberty, or property without due process of the law or to deny any person within its jurisdiction the equal protection of the laws.[57]

Due Process is one of the most sacred and fundamental instruments students and parents can use to fight education injustice. In this sense, due process permits students and parents to challenge education principles set forth by school districts, and to challenge outcomes carried out in urban school classrooms. In a nutshell, it is about students and parents being treated fairly. Even more important, it is about the urban student being adequately educated. Often, parents are under the misperceived

Time for Due Process

notion that their students lose all their rights once they enter onto public school grounds. This is partly true. Students do have a responsibility to behave properly, and to not disrupt the learning process. But they do not have to settle for less than adequate education. Parent's urban students should not have to settle for less than challenging work. They should not have to settle for school principles and practices that are not designed to educate students that grow up in socially and economically depressed communities.

When Carlotta Walls and eight other black students, known as the "Little Rock Nine," walked up the stairs of Little Rock Central High School on September 25, 1957, all they wanted was to make it to class.[58] "But the journey ... would lead the nation on an even longer and much more turbulent path, one that would challenge prevailing attitudes, break down barriers, and forever change the landscape of America."[59] The landscape of public education has certainly changed. Some integration, yes, but more "white flight" to private schools, leaving blacks to create and clone what are known as urban public-schools.

Brown v. Board and the 14th amendment had enlightened the hearts, minds and souls of whites in American culture. But although many believed equality in education would never be equal without integration, there were just as many who hated and detested the idea of black equality. President Bill Clinton writes, "I lived fifty miles away in Hot Springs, Arkansas, and although I had never attended school with black children, I supported integration and was pulling for those kids" [and] so were my parents and grandparents.[60] Before *Brown*, the

14th amendment existed but still blacks were not afforded the same education, social, political, and economic opportunity. "Centuries of institutional norms that had kept Jim Crow at the head of his class do not crumble overnight with one defiant bang of a judicial gavel [thus] *Browns* legacy remains at the center of race relations and educational politics 50 years later."[61] So, as you can see, America had already assaulted blacks by not adhering to the principles expressed in the 14th Amendment.

In 1983, President Ronald Reagan asked his Department of Education to set up a commission to study America's public education system. Reagan learned that there was a continual decline in the quality of public education students received.[62] President Reagan's commission entitled the report, "A Nation at Risk." President Reagan told his commission "there are few areas of American life as important to our society, to our people, and to our families, as our schools and colleges." Almost forty years later, and public education still is not living up to that commission's dire and alarming report. This again is why I believe that states and urban public schools are violating the fourteenth amendment.

The 14th amendment to the U.S. Constitution holds that states must provide due process and equal protection to those with life, liberty, or property interest. Urban school students have a liberty and property interest in their public education. I ask, what is more important than students right to a liberty and property interest. I surmise, none. Thomas Jefferson wrote, "We hold these truths to be self-evident, that all men are created equal, that they are endowed by their Creator with certain unalienable

Rights, that among these are Life, Liberty, and the pursuit of Happiness."

Public education is a liberty right because education expands liberty. It expands liberty because it helps students not just to see their present circumstances, but to see their potential. This is why liberty is important because it stifles an urban student's ability or chance to pursue his happiness. Without the ability to pursue liberty, it tramples the urban student's ability to pursue his ideas, goals, and dreams. Yes, this idea of a liberty interest is abstract. No, liberty cannot be touched. Liberty is a feeling. But, although you know it when you feel it, you also know it when you see it. See, the problem is this, many students that attend urban schools, do not see liberty, or realize its importance. What is worst is not being able to understand that true liberty leads to the acquisition of property, or a property interest.

To pursue happiness, also includes the right to freely pursue property. Property does not just mean to acquire things. It is not just about owning a home, car, business, or boat. These things can be taken at any moment. There are no guarantees in life, especially when it comes to stuff. No, this property right I refer to is the right to learn and learn how to think. The right to immerse yourself in the academic process. The right to see the world differently than yesterday. The right to make a difference by curing incurable diseases or writing a worthy Nobel Peace Prize exposition. See, this property cannot be sold for any sum of money. This property right cannot be traded on the stock market, but this property right can always be invested. It matures as time evolves, and it matures because your education bank continues to expand. This property I allude to is education.

Nevertheless, parents do not just deserve procedural due process, but substantive due process as a tool to challenge urban school education policies. Procedural due process simply means that the government cannot take certain actions against you, without giving you an opportunity to defend governmental action. To demonstrate, after a student enters the school building, her purse is immediately taken for no apparent reason, and without notice. This could be an illegal taking and would absolve the student of an opportunity of due process. Alone those same lines, urban students are being robbed of their future, which I submit is a property interest right. This right is a contestable one that parents and students have more than the legitimate right to fight. This right is substantive in nature and requires procedural due process and procedural mechanisms to fight this form of injustice.

Substantive due process simply means that state actors cannot pass and enact laws that unfairly treat individuals based on their race, religion, gender or ethnicity. I would argue that by failing to implement academic practices that are necessary to motivate students from economically destressed communities, urban schools are violating substantive due process requirements. I admit, the argument is tenuous at best but as I was taught in law school, you always argue in the alternative without establishing meritless and legally baseless claims that are unsupportable.

Unfortunately, urban schools are enacting de facto laws. These types of laws are not actually written. Instead, these are actions taking over time that become an act as presumed law. In this sense, when a school principal places more emphasis on teaching to the test, rather making certain that students are learning material that is relative to the test, this is a de facto law. Or, when an urban school strategically decides to get rid of a mentoring program because it finds it more effective to spend time teaching students the test. Again, this is a de facto law.

Is there a difference between a segregated school and a desegregated school that deliberately fails to inspire, motivate, and educate students that clearly require different teaching methods outside the academic immersion process? If I had to make an educated and informed decision, my answer is no. No there is not a difference. Money and resources are not the answer to inspiring urban students to immerse themselves in the education process. Social and civic engagement is the key to helping students who often grow up in less than favorable social or economic conditions to enthusiastically engage the academic process.

Think about learning this way. As adults, do we mindlessly complete tasks without an end-result in mind? Of course, we do not. That would be absurd. But we expect urban students to respect and to eagerly immerse themselves in the education process without understanding why. Students who attend urban schools' rebel against the process because they do not understand the end game. Students think they will be young forever, and life will not eventually slap their faces with difficult challenges. This is called insanity. Not insanity on the part of the students, but administrators and teachers that fail to do more than teach material students fail to master.

I am reminded of a teacher that clearly instructed us

constantly that the real world begins after high school. As I thought about this one day, I was in the gym with a couple friends that also remembered her pontificating this idea constantly to know end. To that point—we agreed that this unending deliberation to make certain we got it was all she did. As we engaged the topic deeper with intellectual curiosity, we realized something else—that is, she failed to explore and examine the particulars of the real world. We concluded that we had no idea what that statement meant because in our young minds, we were already living in the real world. But as it turned out, the real world as she predicted did exist. My point is this. Urban schools and its leaders cannot take for granted what urban students already know. It is often the case urban students do not know.

Urban schools must change their means to achieve the end. What do I mean? They must change the designed process. They must focus first on teaching students about social responsibility. Urban students resist the academic process because they do not have a foundation on why the education immersion process is so critical. But when jails are built as part of the capitalism paradigm, those jails must be filled. Filled with whom is the question. Students that lack understanding of the processes they must go through after high school graduation, if they graduate.

Parenting and proper role models are key to student success without question. But often, parents drop the ball and constructive roles models are slim in economically depressed communities. Students see destruction and immoral behavior as common. However, urban schools need consistent mentoring programs for these students, and social reformation organizations that teach the importance of programs that will reduce dependency. As early as middle school, urban students know what government assistance programs are, and how those programs can help them someday. This is a harsh reality, but true. I can remember sometimes when my mother had to resort to what is culturally known as food stamps. She admirably told me to always be ashamed of them. In fact, she would not allow me to spend them because of the stigma associated. The fact that she would make certain that I would not grow up depending on governmental handouts has been key to my success. But it also taught me something else. It taught me to see myself superior, and not inferior.

Yes, due process gives students and parents the inherent right to fight against institutional forces that seek to deprive students of what fundamentally belongs to them. It is not just about students who grow up in distressed communities having the right to learn. It is about them being able to see the invaluable benefits of learning. It is about them recognizing that learning does not have to be engaged as some boring, unattractive thing to do. It is about teaching them their respective roles in society, and how they will help construct, shape, and mold society. More important, it is about them absolutely realizing that they have a responsibility not only to educate themselves, but to add value to society, and to share that value of education with future students.

I am again reminded of the great Dr. Martin Luther King. His words and speeches constantly spring from my heart, which allow me to focus on urban education's current state of affairs. Kings words were prolific and described the new negro's sense of urgency to achieve social and political equality. He wrote, "the crisis has been precipitated, on the other hand, by the radical change in the Negro's evaluation of himself. There would probably be no crisis in race relations if the Negro continued to think of himself in inferior terms and patiently accepted injustice and exploitation."

We needed yesterday, urban schools to help students to reevaluate themselves to realize their self-worth. We need urban students to become angry. Angry about the radical approach administrators and teachers have taken in teaching. It is radical in my opinion to continue to fail students because of a bias. Some teachers believe students are hopeless because of their background or who their parents are. I have personally had teachers tell me that they focus less on certain students because of a student's last name. What hope do blameless urban students have when they are not giving a fair chance because of their given last name. It is one thing to fight injustice because of hidden forces, but because of your last name is sickening.

Injustice accurately depicts what too many urban schools have ushered as a mandate for students that society counts to fail. I am tearing up just thinking about the students that have no hope. Sometimes this hope is eternal because of poorly executed jobs by urban schools. The urban students that prisons are counting on to fail. This is an American tragedy. In a country rich as the United States, this should not be. Urban students need help to see themselves differently. They need to see their value, even when their circumstances may symbolize that they have nothing to value. This chapter is about audacity. I need urban schools to have the audacity to serve the urban student's best interest. I need parents to not sit on the side lines and continue to permit educational injustice to be carried out in their communities. This is a fight that is worth having. This is the new civil rights struggle. This is a cause that we all must die empty to solve. We must thrust our entire being to shed light on this issue. Think of it this way, every time a baby is born into an urban community, she is already marked with hopeless despair. Her chances at a fair shake in life are diminished because of the urban school she must attend.

Chapter 11
Let Your Voices Be Heard

"So much of our turbulent history—the stain of slavery an anguish of civil war; the yoke of segregation and tyranny of Jim Crow; the death of four little girls in Birmingham; and the dream of a Baptist preacher—all that history met on this bridge. When the trumpet call sounded for more to join, the people came—black and white, young and old, Christian and Jew, waving the American flag and singing the same anthem full of faith and hope."[63]

I remember my first day as a substitute teacher. I was ready to go in and dictate the lessons of the day. Not to my surprise, I had no problem demanding and earning respectable behavior from my urban students. But it was more than just that. After teaching several classes that day, I learned something critical. I learned that urban students from very similar backgrounds as I, desired to learn so long as they were inspired. So long as you related to them and shared your story, they were eager to engage the process. I was fascinated to learn that urban students with behavior problems desired to learn and cared to listen to what I had to say. Quickly, I knew that the student was not the problem,

Let Your Voices Be Heard

it was the teacher.

Years later, I was invited to career day to speak to several urban students in several classrooms. As you can imagine, I saw some wonderful things and met some awesome teachers. But I also witness some unfortunate incidents that were not surprising. On this particular day, this class was held by a substitute teacher. After walking in, I immediately knew that the students were in control, and she was too comfortable watching them do as they saw fit.

I walked in and said, "hello."

They responded with nothing, as I didn't speak.

I didn't fret because I constantly work with these types of students, and I use to be just as they were, I thought to myself.

I spoke once more, "hello, my name is Mr. McCullough, how are you today?"

This time, a couple students responded.

Okay, I had had enough. I shouted with fierce rage, "this is unacceptable, and I will not tolerate it."

Many looked at me with contempt. It didn't matter.

Many of their faces were twisted sideways as I had just violated some unspoken or unhidden code.

At that moment, one young lady reminded standing combing another young girl's hair.

I know what you are thinking, did I want to slap her on that floor where she stood, of course I did, but societies' norms wouldn't permit it.

"Excuse me young lady, what is your name," I inquired.

"None of your business," she spoke.

"Okay none of your business, can you please have a seat?"

With determined hesitation, she eventually sat!

"Thank you."

"Now, let's try this again."

"My name is Mr. McCullough and I'm going to talk to you about the study of law and some important civil and human rights cases."

As I spoke, many students engaged in sidebar conversations. A few were very attentive, but not enough. My deliberate, caring tone transitioned into one that exhibited tumultuous anger and disgust. As politely and stern as I could, I blurted out, "this does not make any sense—the level of disrespect many of you have for authority right now."

Although at that moment, I was livid with many of them—I also knew it wasn't their fault. They were mere products of their home and school environments. Yes, they were acting out, but they also needed guidance and direction. As I have repeatedly argued in this book, urban students must be trained to value education and the education process. Without this important aspect achieved—the urban student cannot be seriously engaged in the academic setting. That moment with them proved my point as I was already aware. Not am I only aware, but so are teachers and administrators that work in urban school districts.

Martin Luther King eloquently wrote "I Have A Dream"

speech. If you are curious why I am harping over King's words and my dire need to continue to express his rhetoric, allow me to explain. Like King recognized the need for social and economic equality for blacks. I also have the same overwhelming passion for education equality for students that attend urban schools. King believed one day that his children would be judge by the content of their character, not the content of their skin. I fiercely desire that all students can receive an adequate education, not because of where they live or don't live, or not because of how much wealth their parents have amassed, or the amount of political clout their parents have. No, I pray someday that urban school students will be educated fairly because it is a fundamental constitutional right in this country.

Although this is my prayer. Prayer and desire alone are not enough. Action is needed. Voices are required. Platforms are necessary. This must be a social movement. A movement like the "Black Lives Matter." According to Abu-Jamal, the "Black Lives Matter" movement exist because of "manifestations of solidarity and resistance [that] give voice to the eruption of outrage, angst, hopes, and insurgent protest provoked by each new killing."[64] A movement for the students, for the parents, by the students, by the parents. I am not advocating civil disobedience, of course. I am not suggesting that urban students attend schools and disrupt the academic and instructional process. No, this is the type of civil unrest that many totalitarian countries engage.

That said, urban students have the fundamental right not to be associated with certain ideas, ideologies, beliefs or practices. This right, I believe is embedded and protected in the First Amendment to the U.S. Constitution. In *West Virginia State Board of Education v. Barnette*, Justice Jackson expressed that students could not be compelled or forced to salute the flag. He cautioned that we are a nation that does not think or gestured in conformity to accepted ideals and norms.[65] In 1958, Justice Harlan put it this way, "the freedom of association is an independent right [that] possesses an equal status with the other rights specifically enumerated in the First Amendment."[66] We must broadly think about this issue that plagues urban schools. We must view these urban institutions as large bodies that prescribe to sets of academic norms that are outside of the mainstream. I know this is a broad and theoretical statement that may lack full clarity. Put it this way, urban students are not being forced or compelled to salute the American flag, but they endorse daily failing urban education practices and policies that undoubtedly will ill-prepare them for post-secondary education and adulthood.

What about the spirit of intellectualism? What does it mean to be an intellect? An intellect is someone considered thoughtful and engages in critical thinking, research, and reflection on society and proposes solutions for those problems. Think about that for a moment. It seems to me that an intellect is someone who understands a great part of his existence is to challenge the status quo and seek out ways to solve some of this nation's pressing problems. For years because of my urban education— my understanding of the larger world was hindered, and I was considered a subjugated thinker. I was raped of the broader understanding of the importance of learning. I wasn't conscious that knowledge was critical to shape, mode, and frame a concept of the type of world that would help to promote democracy and fairness.

Many urban students are subjugated thinkers. They are clueless as to what happens outside of urban corridors. They think differently as I did. They don't have any clue about credit, finances, savings, social issues surrounding unfair pay or women's reproductive rights, institutional norms, civic engagement, and many more issues. Why do I articulate this? Because if they lack understanding of these often, sophisticated problems—it is no way they will be able to fix them. As a result, urban students remain conformed thinkers and ideal candidates for prison and government payrolls.

During the civil rights era, King developed what was known as the peaceful non-resistance movement. The movement focused on highlighting to the country in a non-violent, but peaceful manner that blacks deserve the right to share the same rights as whites. They sat at lunch counters with other whites when it was illegal. They marched and protested injustices that only targeted blacks. The freedom riders travel to the deep south with keen awareness of the danger they could face. These nonviolent protests were about securing the type of freedoms required to achieve the American dream. Blacks only wanted what whites were able to enjoy. They wanted to vote, integrate into schools, restaurants, and to walk down the street not in fear. But what they also wanted was adequately funded public schools and the ability to send their kids to a white school if desired. The civil liberties and freedoms sought then were on a larger scale, but the right to a quality urban education should be a fundamental right that demands an outcry by parents, students, teachers, politicians and every stakeholder that has the audacity to give a dam.

We are a land of freedom and democracy. Because of our democratic society, we have the right to shed light on injustice. If you ask me, this is the worst type of injustice an urban student can face. Urban teachers sheer disregard for the social, civic, economic, and criminal injustices that urban students undoubtedly will face may not be literal killings that gave rise to the "Black Lives Matter" movement, but certainly, it reflects an extinction of future black and brown communities. An extinction that will occur because of a lack of black education and a misunderstanding of the social dynamics that plague black and brown communities.

Think of it this way, Rosa Parks refused to give her seat up to a white man because she was tired of the unequal treatment. She remained seated on the principle that she had a fundamental right to enjoy the same rights and privileges as the white man. Martin Luther King and others suggested the easiest way to precipitate indiscriminate social change was through economic behavior. As a result, blacks boycotted the bus industry by not using the system. This caused a reduction in the bus system's revenue, therefore, granting blacks the equal right to sit anywhere on the bus. An important lesson may be drawn from this strategic scenario that urban school students and parents can use.

That said, public schools receive funds based on the number of students that are enrolled and attend school. A movement of this magnitude would have to be strategically planned, and it will take almost one hundred percent buy-in by all urban students and parents. The opponents will try to argue that this hurts the student because every day she is absent, she fails to learn. I would argue, every day she attends, she is not learning what is required anyway. To this point, the best way to bring awareness to this issue, and to acquire change, is to impact urban school's economic bottom line.

It is important to remember that school administrators and teachers work for students and parents. There is this false sense of entitlement by urban school administrators because they have a right to control corridors and classrooms. Yes, this is true. They do have an ultimate responsibility to ensure schools are safe environments for students. But this does not erase the fact that urban students deserve a fair and adequate education. This does not mean that it is fair for school administrators to group students based on their academic capacity, or to group them based on their less than satisfactory disciplinary track record. Why do you think this is done? Have you ever heard of the phrase, "birds of a feather flock together?" I am sure you have. In this instance, kids are forced to be grouped with like-minded students that already fight against the system. These are just some of the problems. Urban schools make the unfortunate calculation that they will lose an unspecified number of students to urban community societal problems, so why not focus on the urban students that have a chance at success.

If something is going to be done by these types of unfair practices, students and parents must veto by not attending school. Is this radical? Yes, but these are radical and desperate times that cause for desperate measures. Parents and students must demand education equality. Certainly, they may be unaware of what that looks like. It does not matter. First, bring attention to what you believe is unequal and unfair. And if you do, I promise education reformers will help in your cause. See, if you ask me, many education reformers have given up because they don't see parents and students fight for what is right and fight for their own future. But the reformers are out there ready to do whatever, it takes to reform outdated overt and covert policies that are not designed to educate urban school students.

By no means am I suggesting that this movement will be popular or easy. In fact, I am sure that it will be difficult. If history has taught us anything, fighting for justice is never easy. Advocating what is principally right is tough. Being on the right side of justice and at the right time, always seems unlikely. But significant adversity just symbolizes that the few who desire to keep the status quo intact, is on the brink of losing the battle. I was always told when times are tough, you exemplify an even tougher exterior. The road for social justice is never easy. This is exactly about social justice. Adequate education is not only a human right, it is a civil right.

Blacks realized education as a true civil right after the passage of *Brown v. Board*. However, although the force of law recognized the inherent inequality of segregated schools, the law has not recognized the inherent inequality in education among urban school students in contrast to suburban public schools where tax dollars are unequal, or where parents have more time and resources to help their students.

What am I talking about here? You may be under the impression that I am talking about American students being able to compete with students from other countries. No, because in order to compete, there must be adequate competition. Urban school student's ability to compete is ideal. Instead, I am talking about survival. Yes, surviving gang violence, teenage pregnancy, sexual transmitted diseases, jail sentences, and poverty.

Sometimes, I believe education is frowned upon in urban schools and communities. The students spend all their non-school hours, gaming, chatting, watching countless hours of television. The students barely read and will quickly tell you that they hate to read. Have you ever heard the old saying, "if you want to hide something from someone, put it in a book?" In this media crazed society, teens spend every waking hour hovering in front of a television becoming less informed and intrigued by the prospect of educational attainment. A radical shift needs to occur among urban students. This is the only true way to change urban school student's mentality and philosophy about education.

I don't just believe, but I know these students don't just deserve better, but the best. These students are missing out on the God given right and opportunity to dream, to believe in themselves and the possibilities that their future holds. You tell me, what is right about robbing young people of their destiny. Robbing them of the right to think or dream big. Forcing them into a life that is destined for not greatness, but failure. This is shameless, and the schools that are acutely aware of the harm and danger committed daily by their school policies, deserve to be close.

Put yourself in these young people shoes or their parents. I don't know about you, but it hurts to think that urban students have no clue what lies ahead. All the disappointment, heart throbbing pain and undesirable circumstances. For many of these students, life is going to beat them into the dirt. Why? Because these schools cop out. Cop out of fighting for their student's hopes, dreams, and potential. Just think about the severity of those words. By no measure is it fair. This is why I believe it is time for urban students and parents to rise to their feet. Let their voices be heard from the state legislatures, from the mayor front doorsteps, to the hallways of the school superintendent's office.

In this moment, I am reminded of Jekalyn Carr's hit single, "Greater is Coming." But greater isn't coming for urban students after graduation—presuming he graduates. A new life of sheer disappointment and pity partying he can expect. He will struggle with endless days and nights to understand why life seems to seek to defy his existence until he is unable to fight another day. Not only has the urban student been pushed out of a system unprepared for post-secondary education—he has been forced into a society that unfortunately is not colorblind. He will have to learn that many social and institutional norms are put in place to make his life tougher. Because the urban student has been pushed out inadequately prepared, he will resort to many vices. Unfortunately, many of those vices will push him into a system of repeated incarceration. All that said, this is why urban parents and students cannot afford not to be heard. Sound your trumpets to bring the type of political and emotional awareness that is needed to help fix this God forsaken issue. During your moments of doubtfulness or will to bring forth social justice to urban students, remember that democracy has never been conquered overnight and there are powers in numbers. But even more important, parents and other stakeholders that believe their voices must be heard—this problem demands your attention because it is much bigger than you. Remember that change comes to those that fight—and those that fight for causes on the right side of history.

It is tempting to articulate that we are a nation built on fairness, but this assertion is farthest from the truth. We as a nation can sometimes express intolerable views and dissent because of selfish motives. We can conclude that our selfish desire stems from a place of always wanting or craving for self. This is a natural tendency to want the best or be the best because this country teaches hard work and sacrifice are the ultimate keys to success. However, it chooses not to candidly express its flaws. Because this nation refuses to express the truth—even when it hurts or is embarrassed, justice seekers must fight and stand up for equality for all. We are a great nation because of unselfish acts by brave people. This is the true testimony of our greatness and how we have overcome significant racism, segregation, and bigotry in this country. So long as we exist, bad people and policies will exist. The silver-lining is this—courageous people that believe in the decency of humanity is necessary to safeguard democracy will continue to eradicate the bad that seeks to trump good.

Chapter 12
Teachers Must Fill the Gaps

Quality teaching includes engaging students in active learning, creating intellectually ambitious tasks, using multiple teaching modalities, assessing student learning and adapting to the learning needs of the students, creating supports, providing clear standards, reflection, and opportunities for revision and developing a collaborative atmosphere is strengthened by a strong student-teacher relationship.[67]

There is a central argument that centers around students lacked achievement. Teachers, support staff, and administrators all agree that parents must and should do a better job if urban students are to succeed. I will be first to only agree that parents need to do better, but it is not imperative in order for these students to succeed. The argument is flawed, and I will express why my position is such.

When parents abuse children, the state steps in, takes kids, investigates, and releases findings to decide whether the child should be taken permanently, or for some period until the parent can clean up her act. That makes sense because we want to protect children from abusive parents, and to ensure their help and safety is not in jeopardy.

Second case and point, if a parent leaves a young kid unattended in the car or in home, and the child subsequently is injured, authorities will step in and may charge, and convict the parent depending on the type of neglect or nature of the crime. The same principle applies. The goal is to protect the child from any harm or danger. At this point, I imagine you see where I am going with this argument.

So, the law has imposed a set of moral obligations and duties on parents that requires them to be responsible caretakers. Apparently, parents as caretakers does not include the promotion and development of student's academic growth. However, since states seemingly believes parents have a choice not to get involve in their kid's education, schools must do more to bridge the gap. Until states make it a punishable offense for parents to take an offhands approach to their kid's educational welfare, teachers and staff must fill the gap.

Let me be clear, I am not advocating for a policy that sanctions or penalizes parents for their lack of parental involvement in their child's education. I am simply pressing the point that schools must do more when parents do less. It is no secret that many urban parents take an offhands approach for different reasons. It is also important to remember that all parents do not take this approach. I do not want to over inflate or conflate the facts. That is not, nor will it ever be my intention for writing this book. I will deal with facts and make strong logical inferences throughout this book only.

I have argued tooth and nail that this is the only way forward to achieve academic progress in urban schools. Teachers must take an aggressive proactive approach to filling the gaps, where parents drop the ball. I am not suggesting only teachers. This must be a school-wide community approach. To this point, school leadership must adopt this approach, granting teachers its permission, and providing necessary training to facilitate this holistic approach. Fixing the problems in urban schools are doable. "For too long we approached education policy decisions by pitting the interests of the adults in the system—the school boards, the union leaders, the textbook manufacturers, the charter operators—against one another[thus] the special interest won, and the students lost."[68]

Teachers and administrators contend that if we focus on value building, we will not have time to teach. If we spend time being the parent, we cannot be the teacher. If we do the parent's jobs, what will the parent do. These are the types of arguments less passionate teachers like to articulate. If you ask me, if you are not willing to embrace teaching beyond its traditional role, you should not be in a classroom. Urban schools must take the approach that we cannot only be focus on student excellence but raising the expectations of teachers. A student will not be successful if she doesn't have a quality teacher in the classroom. Take for example what a teacher does in his Philadelphia seventh grade classroom that is primarily African American. Herman Douglas, "You're great!" Each student responds, "I'm great." That is what every student hears from Mr. Douglas when they enter his classroom at Mary McLeod Bethune Elementary School in a neighborhood of North Philadelphia plagued with crime, violence, and poverty.[69] Douglas went on to say that "it is his mission to save as many students as possible." Douglas further noted, "I have been that child under the desk crying because my father was not around, and I know what it's like when you want nice sneakers, a nice car ... and you don't have any of those things and you have to think about stealing it."

Teachers are paid to do more than teach. Hold on before you go on this long tirade, shouting expletives at this book. I did not say teachers are fairly and adequately paid. That is another debate that needs and must be had in every state legislature in the United States. Point remains, you took an oath that you will provide students with all the academic support and assistance needed. However, without addressing this issue of teacher pay too much, I certainly believe that teachers should be paid adequately. But not a system that just awards a teacher based on tenure, it has been proven repeatedly to be ineffective. Teachers should be paid based on their added value, similar to athletes, but definitely not to the degree of unfairness one player is paid to another. That system has ruined society and how capitalism should operate. But teachers should be paid more. How else do you expect to attract some of the best minds to teach urban students.

That aside, the academic assistance urban schools attempt to provide is flawed. Many urban students come through your doors not ready nor excited to learn for varying reasons. Let's not focus on the causes but focus on the reality that the causes exist. Principal Jamina Clay-Dingle, who has made it a point to recruit black men to her classrooms says, "we have a lot of children where they have moms at home, they have grandma, but they don't have dad, and uncles are not around.[70] For a moment, think about being an employed adult, and your employer has reminded you several instances that you cannot bring your problems to work. Your employer requires that you leave all external and internal problems outside the workplace in order to effectively perform.

I am not certain about you, but for me that would be a tall task. Frankly, I ask you to seriously reflect on moments when you just could not adjust, adapt, and focus on your employment duties. Everyone has experienced this episode. If you say you have not, respectfully, I think you are fabricating. Putting that into proper perspective, if supposedly, mature, prudent adults have battled with this issue, I ask, why do you assume urban students can somehow separate their personal lives from their academic lives. I am not suggesting teachers be counselors and psychologists. That would be absurd. In so many words, Morris captures what this chapter is truly about.

She writes in that the drive to cast contemporary America as a "colorblind society impairs [urban schools] ability to recognize two important phenomena: the persistence of segregation and how it shapes the identities of [urban students], and the impacts of systems that reproduce and reinforce unequal access to educational opportunity. No institution is immune to these forces. But our schools are the places that have just as much (arguably more) influence as any other social factor on how children understand themselves personally and in relation to the world around them. Schools are, not surprisingly, one of the largest influences on the life trajectory of [urban students.]" [71]

But I do believe teachers and support staff must be cognizant and put forth the type of empathy that sympathizes with urban student's apparent problems, even if you are unaware of the specific problem. Why continue to teach at the student, rather teach the student. My tenure as a teacher was invigorating, and never daunting. Never daunting because I understood how high the stakes were.

Shifting unnecessary blame on the parents is not helpful to our students. Shifting blame does not solve the problem. In fact, it only permits this ridiculous persistence of the status quo. Students fail, teachers fail, schools continue to under-educate, and urban communities continue to spiral down roads of vicious crime and poverty.

I have a simple message for teachers and staff that play this game of Russian Roulette, either cease it, or immediately dropped out of the profession. I like to equate teacher's duties to our American soldiers who tirelessly put their lives on the line for this country. They do it because of what the U.S. flag represents. The American flag symbolizes hope, freedom, democracy and prosperity. Similarly, teachers in urban schools have an immense responsibility to help students realize hope is eternal, freedom is more than ideal, democracy is more than a symbolic gesture, and prosperity is gained by realizing, internalizing all these values and exercising them all. These ideals are representative of this nation's value system.

It is presumed that we are a nation of blind justice. That means systems and institutions do not see color, and equality and fairness is evenly distributed. However, I think it is more a hope, than a strong belief. Besides, beliefs are often strongly associated with corroborating facts. But maybe blind injustice is taking place. Because urban schools blindly sabotage student's opportunity to receive and adequate education. Blind injustice because the student's race, gender, or ethnicity does not matter. The urban student's hidden or obvious zeal for learning does not matter, and the system does not care to recognize it. As such, the urban student will quickly adapt to the school's culture and say what the heck. These are brazen assertions, but reality in too many urban schools.

If you think I make these criticisms with simple thought, think again. Each word I express is made with careful consideration, but you must remember this is my truth, and many other's truth as well. Until you experience it or research it, do not jump to conclusions. This is not about feelings. Far too long I have spared feelings about the insensitivity, and indifference urban teachers and administrators demonstrate daily. Urban schools are rated "D" and "F" consistently. How could you conclude anything other than urban schools are assaulting the 14th amendment to the Constitution?

Teachers and administrators should look at their job as a gatekeeper to learning. You get to decide daily will you help urban students become a better person. You get decide if you will teach them something that is not related to the test. You get to decide if you will find time to start a program that focuses on life skills or civic engagement. You get to decide if you are going to find ways to get additional resources, or just say it is not your problem. These are simple questions, but difficult decisions

Teachers Must Fill the Gaps

to make. I get it. I do not just want to bash teachers. That does not help anyone. But I will always speak truth to power.

The saying goes something like this. Never judge a man before you have walked a mile in his shoes, or at least knows his story. Too often, we like to assume that parents just don't give a dam, and deliberately send their kids to school to do their job. Listen, I will be the first to admit excuses are for the weak. But, within many black homes, women are the primary caretaker, and the father is absent. Mothers must work two and three jobs to support her child. I have amazing female friends that must be at work as early as 5 a.m. in the morning. Their children must get themselves up, dressed, and out of the house to catch the bus alone.

My mother was a single parent that worked several jobs to support my sister and me. My mother also instilled the value of education. However, my mother just did not have the time to help me with homework, to make sure I did homework, or to make sure I was routinely reading. This did not make her an unconcerned parent. This just meant she was too busy working to provide shelter, clothing, and food for her children.

Many urban parents leave one job just to punch the clock at a second one. Often, urban parents attended urban schools, and desperately desire their kids to have a brighter future than theirs. Maybe I am too optimistic, but I just believe the average parent desires the best for their child.

There are bad people in every industry. In an ideal world, all teachers would be sophisticated, avid learners that love to teach even under some of the direst situations. But we know this is not the case. We also know that there are bad parents that refuse to educate their kids outside of the classroom. I also think there is a misperception about parents educating students. I think sometimes teachers expect parents to help students with their homework, and sometimes parents think they must help their students with their homework. I believe both beliefs are misguided.

Teaches must not assume that all parents can help their students with any subject. They must not also assume that parents can afford to pay for additional academic support. But more important, I think parents must understand that they are not required to help their students with homework, nor should they be ashamed.

However, what parents must first understand is teaching their kids to value education. It would be ideal if parents could model this, but not required. Parents must merely insist their students do homework, read, and study. This sounds simple but is not. Parents must develop an action plan, schedule, and daily enforce and reinforce these habits.

Teachers must enforce and reinforce what parents are also doing at home. Yes, this is what occurs in some of the best public schools. I make this point because if teachers learn how to communicate to parents how simple their job is, maybe more parents will step up to the plate. Remember, this chapter is about teachers filling the gap.

Think about it. Teachers can fill the gap most effectively this way. They will see an increase in parent-student participation. Students will see a difference in their parents, parents will see a difference in their students, teachers will recognize a difference in the students; more important, students will realize the difference and believe in themselves, and their abilities.

Essentially, I am alluding to responsibility. Every year elementary teachers will advise students to be responsible for their own learning because middle school teachers will expect them to be independent learners on day one. Middle school teachers will also encourage their students to be academically responsible, resourceful, and independent thinkers because their high school teacher will demand it. High school teacher will give the same advice to their students and tell them no one will hold your hand in college or life.

Obviously, there is something wrong with this picture. We are asking a group of urban students that lack discipline, structure, academic focus, and an understanding for the importance of serious academic engagement to be responsible. Why not just throw the student in a pool and say teach yourself how to swim? Precisely, it doesn't sound wise does it. This is a sheer way to maximize a student's chance of failure.

That isn't to say that some students in urban schools don't follow this advice by their teachers. Remember this book takes a holistic snapshot of urban schools. That means that although there are some tremendous things accomplished in urban schools, the goal is to magnify the serious problems within the context of the 14th amendment. I ask that you engage this text from that perspective because I am afraid you will loosely follow my arguments and make false illogical assumptions about my motive.

Asking a student to be responsible, seeks a student's response to a given instruction. When teachers give homework, the assumption is the urban student will return to school with the lesson complete. When a student has an amount of time to complete a project, the assumption remains that the urban student will complete the assignment. When an urban student has been provided with material to study for an exam, the assumption remains the same. However, how do and how should teachers respond when assumptions are just that, assumptions?

Do teachers fail students for being irresponsible or lazy? Too often, urban students are failed when they don't respond to mandates or instructions accordingly. This is not right and is opposite to filling the gaps. Schools must take steps to help urban students change their attitudes. Urban schools cannot sit by and hope that parents will help their students learn responsibility. Urban schools must require students to attend tutoring sessions, require them to finish homework at school, require them to take tests until a proficient grade is achieved.

This is a deep resemblance of what genuine teacher character looks like when urban schools refuse to let students fail. This is the type of passion that must exude in urban schools in order for these schools to save lives. These students must not be given options to be responsible and must not be given the option to not seriously engage the academic process.

I remember the first time I realized I had the capacity to memorize large sums of information. As a 11th grader, Ms. Wells left an indelible mark on my life. That entire year she pushed me to think outside of the box, and to challenge myself. It was an incredible feeling. She was a teacher who did not see student's limitations. She did not care if your mother or father was an educator or someone of status. She cared about teaching, sharing her knowledge, sharing her passion, and helping students to see the benefit of taking the education process serious.

This is what filling in the gap looks like. What bothers me is, I do not know if this can be taught or learned. I am afraid that these sorts of teachers just have what you call the "it factor." It is comparable to any profession and any person. You cannot explain it. The person just has a natural ability and tendency to be exceptional, and always seek to do more than the job requires.

Teachers must take an approach and demonstrate an attitude of selfless service. For many of these students, they will first encounter structure, discipline, guidance and this feeling that someone actually cares and takes interest in what they do or don't do in school.

As a substitute teacher for more than 5 years, I learned that kids respected teachers that were not afraid to command respect, but also showed them respect. I learned that they respected teachers that loved learning and shared their passion for learning. I learned that if you take the time out to get to know students, you will learn that many of them grow up in difficult home environments. But what you will also learn is that they want to escape these places, and sometimes school is that only outlet.

While in the school system, I purchased shoes, clothes, backpacks, video games, and gave student's money. I remember talking to elementary kids in my classroom about what did they get for Christmas, and some would tell me nothing. Many kids would wear one pair of shoes the entire year. Many also wore unclean uniforms. These types of things devastate kids. So, I would make it my business to provide support when I was able.

I remember as a student in elementary, middle, and high school, teachers had "teacher pets." I am certain this still exist today. I think the damage done is greater in urban schools. These students sit beside the teacher's desk, run all the teacher's errands, helps teachers grade papers, and a list of other things. But what's worst, all the other students that were not considered smart can't understand how one or a few students received special treatment.

This behavior is unacceptable, and it ruined my self-esteem as a student. I have spoken with many high school classmates and interviewed random participants, and they shared the same sentiment. In fact, a good friend of mine, insisted I mention this in my book. So, to you current teachers and future teachers, please get rid of this "teacher's pet" mentality. It hurts significantly more students than it helps. Your job is to develop and improve good self-esteem, not tear it down. No matter the motive or intent, this practice is outdated and significantly harmful.

Coaches you are not going to get away that easily. Urban schools have some of the most extraordinary athletes. In fact, many urban schools recruit them and find ways so they may attend your schools. These students also struggle academically for varying reasons. I am under the strong impression that all students can learn with the right support.

Talented athletes are placed on pedestals and are treated like

Teachers Must Fill the Gaps

royalty throughout high school. Coaches at urban schools buy them clothes, shoes, food, and work diligently to get them into a college program after high school through booster clubs across America. Sounds great right, wrong! You set them up for failure because these athletes are passed alone because of their athletic prowess. Many of these athletes cannot read, and if they can, they cannot interpret what they read. If you have any experience with these schools and athletes, you know that this is the bold unfortunate truth.

The athletes that seemed fortunate to have received a college scholarship to play ball are less fortunate than you can imagine. These athletes typically remain in these programs two years or less. WOW!!! They were treated like livestock just so urban schools could acquire large sums of notoriety while lambasting in their soon short-lived glory. In a whispering moment, it all is taken away. For these athletes, all they were good at was running, catching, or bouncing a ball. They were not told or taught that valuing the education process was connected to athletic success.

The athlete comes back home, finds a minimum wage job or finds himself in and out of jail because the lifestyle that was once given, he cannot provide for himself any longer. He goes through a depression stage because he had no idea people would forget him so quickly. He goes from super stardom to barely recognizable. His life has no meaning. He finds it hard to live and cannot seem to find comfort.

It's no secret that he turns to drugs and alcohol for more than recreational use. He uses it to forget his presence, or to just relive the great moments of the past. It makes sense. Every coach, fan, and family member praised him and likely led him to believe that professional sports were in his future. But these individuals failed to mentor him. They failed to teach him how to separate reality from fiction. The fact is less than one percent of athletes are going to play professional sports.

Coaches your job is to fill gaps where parents are absent. You recruit them, travel with them, guide them, educate them, and mentor them. However, you guide, mentor and teach the wrong things. It takes extraordinary discipline and academic focus for athletes to be successful because their time is so consumed with sports, they must use their unaccounted time wisely.

Your job is to help them build studying and reading habits. Your job is to help them build character. Your job is to help them see beyond their athletic ability. Your job is to give them the facts and help them realize if they don't make it to the big league, options are available. Sadly, these coaches turn their backs, and simply say, he could have made it if he could have left the streets alone, but coaches failed the student by riding the back seat.

I would be remiss if I did not mention the teachers and administrators. You are also culprits because you pass these athletes based on their athletic merit. I attended a school where I saw it first-hand. These athletes were given golden parachutes. Often, they were excused from completing assignments and given grades. The coaches would schedule practice during regular classes, and the administrators and teachers would permit it.

If you ask me, urban schools place focus and emphasis on the wrong things. I get it. The world idolizes athletes and entertainers. But the school must remain committed to what is important and remember why they are there. Your job is to teach, discipline and mentor. Your job is to fill the empty gaps. Just because a few students achieve success, it does not give you a pass.

Think of it like this. Regardless of what you do or don't do as a teacher, some students will succeed with or without you. It is in their DNA. It cannot be explained. But there are not enough of these students in urban schools. There are too many students that desperately need life jackets. These students require your attention, time and focus. They require an extra push and prod. Therefore, I say you must fill the gaps.

Effective teachers take a stance for what is right. Report the bad teachers. Put your jobs on the line. Protest and make your voices heard. Tell your principals that John or Jill must go. Let them know if you don't clean house, I will be forced to resign. Yes, it's just that serious. These students need an advocate. They are unaware that these teachers are destroying their futures by giving them passes. They are blindly unaware because he won't teach, they are being cheated out of an adequate education. You, good teachers, must be vocal protectors of these students from bad teachers. Remember fill gaps and holes where and whenever necessary.

Chapter 13
One Black President, One Thousand Black Inmates

"The distance from Martin Luther King's assassination to Barack Obama's inauguration is a quantum leap of racial progress whose timeline neither cynics nor boosters could predict."[72]

"My suspicion is that more than anything, my election will have affected changes that have already taken place in society: different attitudes about race among a younger generation, greater comfort with diversity in positions of authority,"[73] Obama said to Michael Eric Dyson. Obama went on to say, "I think my election reflected those changes, rather than created them. I'd like to think that my election over time will help consolidate and further fuel greater acceptance of people's differences—a greater appreciation of African American culture."[74] I think as a collective nation, we desire the same view Obama takes, but I'm not quite sure if Obama's election will bring about the type of racial healing necessary to amend the wrinkles of racism. In fact, President Trump's policies and racist rhetoric I believe has threatened democracy and threatened any type of hope for racial reconciliation. History will be the judge. That said, Michelle

Alexander seems to agree with my assessment.

She writes in part that "more African American adults are under correctional control today—in prison or jail, on probation or parole—that were enslaved in 1850, a decade before the Civil War began.... The clock has been turned back on racial progress in America, though scarcely anyone seems to notice. All eyes are fixed on people like Barack Obama and Oprah Winfrey, who have defied the odds and risen to power, fame, and fortune. For those left behind, especially those within prison walls, the celebration of racial triumph in America must seem a tad premature. More black men are imprisoned today than at any other moment in our nation's history. More are disenfranchised today than in 1870, the year the Fifteenth Amendment was ratified prohibiting laws that explicitly deny the right to vote on the basis of race. Young black men today may be just as likely to suffer discrimination in employment, housing, public benefits, and jury service as a black man in the Jim Crow era—discrimination that is perfectly legal, because it is based on one's criminal record. This is the new normal, the new racial equilibrium."[75]

Although Alexander makes strong palpable facts about the conditions of black men in the country and subtle racist institutional tactics that are just undeniable—black success has been realized. This realization is strongly evident by Barack Obama's ascendancy to the highest position in the land. Although a resurgence of hate has resurfaced subsequently due to his win and even more so—after President Trump invaded the White House, this country has witness important and noticeable gains in race relations.

Barack Obama, this nation's 45th president, even more important, this nation's first black president. I can remember his 2008 campaign. You could not explain it, but the time just seemed ripe. White is right, finally seemed to be less relevant than ever. At that moment, the average black American wanted to truly believe that this nation had turned the corner of unspeakable, dangerous bigotry. Unfortunately, not long after Obama's historical win and the perceived social significance of that win, whites around the country were holding their own rallies. But their rallies focused on hate and division. I thought to myself—what does a black person have to do to prove his worth!

But it didn't matter what we do or accomplished—we will never be equal in their eyes.

That night, as articulated by Beverly Tatum, "a series of ugly campus incidents that took place just before and after the election—incidents such as the hanging of an effigy of Barack Obama at the University of Kentucky, the appearance of a noose on a tree at Baylor University, the dumping of a dead bear plastered with Obama posters at Wester Carolina University, and the postelection Facebook post by a University of Texas student that called for all the hunters to gather up, we have a n— in the white house." Why is this important within the urban schools-student's context? Well, my suspicion is that urban students are isolated from current and political affairs that undoubtedly affect them. The urban student has no desire or appetite to fight what they don't see or understand. She is concerned with social media and the number of likes gained, or the latest juicy gossip of the day. I'm not arguing that we should develop a group of cognizant urban students that only focus on race relations. I'm not suggesting we develop urban students that advocate a militant approach. No, I am only saying that urban students must be aware that social change is hard and often resistant. They must understand that the fight for all forms of justice must be fought in order to secure. But the urban student will never achieve this fundamental principle without the right education. Urban schools must educate beyond learning to read and write— yet there are legitimate arguments many of them are failing at doing this basic thing. All that said, I personally believe that this country has beat some insurmountable odds concerning the vestiges of discrimination and segregation, but our foot must remain on the gas pedal. I will reframe from my momentary digression.

As I was saying, it could not be explained but you could tell the time was ripe. Ripe as an apple picked from an apple tree. The seed had been planted, and it finally seemed that the countless Civil Rights icons like Martin Luther King, Jesse Jackson, John Lewis, Medgar Evars, and Al Sharpton led the way so that we could see history in the making. Obama's coolness and suave demeanor helped ride him into the big White castle, known as the white house, and I and other blacks could not be any prouder. This was our moment. It seemed surreal, and I can remember sitting with my wife and kids lamenting and sobbing like a baby. Ironically, these were not tears of despair or frustration, but tears of hope, "Yes we Can," Obama's slogan during his many speeches.[76] The "Yes We Can" slogan suggested a type of surreal prophetic hope for blacks. We finally felt that this nation had accepted us and felt comfortable judging us by the "content of our character," and not by our brown and black skin.

In *"The Black Presidency,"* Michael Dyson writes words expressed by Jeremiah Wright, a pastor emeritus of Trinity United Church of Christ in Chicago. By many in the religious and academic community, Jeremiah is considered a prolific, intellectual that gives profound thought to social issues married with religious principles. Dyson cites Jeremiah saying, "the government gives [blacks] the drugs, builds bigger prisons, passes a three-strike law and then wants us to sing God bless America. No, no, no, God dam America ... for treating our citizens as less than human."[77] I would add, local school districts now even pass political bonds to build even bigger public schools but fail to focus on community redevelopment. The schools are state of the art but are concentrated in impoverished communities. These schools are in the heart of poverty, crime, high teenage pregnancy, drugs, liquor stores, and urban corner-package stores.

I like to make it clear that I do not buy into or espouse Mr. Jeremiah Wrights intense rhetoric per se. But I do sympathize with his motivation to articulate such words. That said, I believe urban school districts with black leaders are damming our urban students to a state of self-degradation and to a position of constant misery, despair, and hopelessness. We need black male hope in this country, and what better way to achieve this than through our education system. We should be our brother's keeper, not our brother's sweeper. Sweeping our students into positions of poverty and incarceration because of unacceptable misguided education.

One Black President, One Thousand Black Inmates

Yes, we had our first black president. The culmination of black success or this idea that any black kid could do anything outside of dribbling a ball was reached or was it. I think we have given this country too much undue credit. Besides, Barack is an interracial American. This fact cannot and should not elude us. Furthermore, many in white America hated the feeling of black supremacy. So, I beg the question, are urban schools truly serving the best interest of our students.

Let us not confuse a moment of perceived culmination by an interracial president with an eradication of bigotry and hate. Urban schools are developing and fostering communities of hopelessness, where government assistance is the right way of life, while hard-work and academic excellence is frowned upon. Urban students are trained for impending incarceration. The question is never if, but when will the next black male be introduced and subdued by a system of advertent slavery. Dyson writes, "King was darker and angrier ... and did not think America would move forward without considerable coercion." Ultimately, King concluded that the Civil Rights Act of 1964 and the 1965 Voting Rights Act did very little to improve [southern] ghettos or to "penetrate the lower depths of Negro deprivation."[78] Some sixty odd years later, urban schools continue to struggle to help their students to leave poverty and ghettos behind.

Obama's presidency was viewed as an eclipse of new hope. It was seen as a way to reduce unfair prison sentences, reduce the number of minorities in prison, and to educate the mis-educated urban student. Of course, these were conversations had by intellectuals and elites. The people that live in these current conditions never saw Obama's ascendency to the White House as a means to reach supremacy in their own lives. Nor did black students truly fathom the true historic nature of Obama's victory, and what his position meant for their future, if it meant anything. All this talk was good banter for the academic and political community to capitalize. Banter in the sense of spirited and intelligent gossip. This is not to say that these issues are not seriously contemplated and addressed by our intellectual and political leaders.

When you take a serious, inquisitive look at urban schools, you cannot help but wonder if King's assassination was in vain. We do not live in a post color-free society where white privilege does not still spread like wild-fires in California alone many corridors of varying institutions. These institutions are core to survival. The criminal justice system, employment organizations, and banks to name a few. These three institutions are the linchpins to social mobility, yet, minorities are yielded unfair jail sentences, unfair pay, and unfair interest rates, that is, if they are approved for a loan.

It is unfortunate that I cannot discuss urban school's assault on the 14th amendment without expressing what many blacks have learned, that is, structural and systemic unfairness in our institutions is alive and prevalent. I mention this point because many of the pitfalls surrounding urban school's blunder are centered around non-disclosure or inadvertent stupidity to not educate urban students about the realities of social inequities and unjust laws. Martin Luther King wrote, "that the central quality in people's lives is pain—pain so old and so deep that it shows in almost every moment of [their] existence."[79] The deep pain of being told to move to the back of the bus is not unconscionable, but our hearts and minds were scared when told niggers can't eat here. These acts of dehumanization were hurtful, but nothing is more devastating and painful than watching our urban student's being pushed into poverty, incarceration, and a systemic life of despair, grief, and hopelessness.

What hurts is this. Black equality is possible, maybe more difficult to achieve, but possible. I am not talking about achieving economic and social equality as black athletes, nor is there something wrong with running, bouncing, or catching a ball. Never mind the institutions that suppress black opportunity and equality. This is a serious issue, but not as serious as the attention we give the issue. As a black father of three boys, I teach my boys about black responsibility and being a black role model. I also teach them that you have to be better and work harder than the competition. I do not want my boys to be deceived by nice or cordial talks by people that look over their potential. Unfairness is alive no matter how hard we seek to escape it. This discourse is the same discourse that is needed in urban schools with our urban students. To otherwise not, is a deliberate downfall by urban institutions.

The dichotomy between successful blacks and blacks incarcerated is not mind boggling. Sure, many people outside of the black or minority race pretend to be perplexed by the issue, but minorities get it. How do you explain the insurgence of minorities that end up in jail, and the less than insurgence of minority success? This is not to undermine the success blacks and other minorities persist to experience, but we cannot pretend that the number of minorities that end up in jail cells isn't a huge problem, and a stain on this country's meaning of democracy.

Fuller writes, "I believe that Mortimer Adler was right when he said there are no unteachable children. What we have are adults who have not figured out how to teach them. Too many of our students are force to stay in schools that do not work for them, and frankly, didn't work for their parents."[80] Fuller is right about two things, these students are forced to stay in these schools and two parents were inadequately educated as well. But I take issue with the assertion that urban school-teachers haven't figured out how to teach urban students. This is a myth. They dam well know how to teach these students but take the approach Fuller articulates. That is, "the message that teachers and schools send to our children is that my paycheck is going to come whether you learn or not."[81] Ask me how many times I heard this as a kid while attending an urban school? The answer is a resounding too many to count or remember. Excuse me as I journey down a narrow path of thinking, but my experiences have zealously led me to believe that too many urban teachers attended urban schools themselves. That isn't to say that teachers educated in urban schools shouldn't teach urban students. In fact, I think these teachers are the best candidates for the position only if they took on a new persona after graduating from an urban school. What do I mean? I mean they must to go through a transformation stage that centers around academic rigor, and a thirst and unparallel desire to soak up knowledge. Why is this important?

Teachers with the urban school backgrounds can be a crucial

factor to building critical rapport among urban school students. I am not suggesting that this is a definite prerequisite. I am merely saying that this requirement alone may help. As a teacher and mentor, it helps me to relate to my students. Helping them to realize their potential by sharing my story to garner my current success was pivotal. But back to this point made earlier by Fuller that urban teachers don't know how to teach urban students is just not true. Too many urban teachers have no business in urban schools for varying reasons. Reasons like I decided to teach because I couldn't find work anywhere else. I graduated with no clue what to do with my life, so why not try teaching. Teaching has to choose you, like preaching I would submit. If you choose it, you will do total and inaccurate justice to the non-calling. Teachers are doing just that. They are committing selfish acts of injustice against our most vulnerable institutions and its students.

Urban school students deserve righteous help and hope by committed adults that seriously desire to change student's lives. However, these urban teachers often fail to go through the transformation stage I mentioned earlier. That is, they never truly embrace the concept of education. They never truly buy into the power of learning. They may hold the title teacher but should be called substitute. Essentially, these teachers never become socially and politically engage adults. They never truly become one with the education process, and its importance. In this book, I talk about students realizing and taking on a new identity. Urban schoolteachers must also take on this new identity in order to help their students realize their true potential and understand their social responsibility. Fuller writes, "only an educated people can be expected to make the type of choices which assert their freedoms and reinforce their sense of social responsibility."[82] Social responsibility implies that individuals have an incredible responsibility to act purposefully to create a just society or community that works for all. It demands teachers to empower urban students and to teach them how to someday empower others as they venture into different paths.

Urban teachers must be different. They must think, look, and act different. They cannot conform to the urban school culture but create the type of culture that sets high expectations for their urban students. In an ideal setting, the hope is all urban teachers will buy into developing a culture that centers around academic rigor, but we know this is far from true. That said, the urban teachers who emphatically understand their mission must work with other like-minded teachers to develop classroom culture that will help shift and redevelop urban student's attitudes and perceptions about academic excellence. Teachers must model learning. She must not be a victim to teaching from the manual. Kids are much smarter than you think. They quickly determine if a teacher knows her material, or just wants the urban student to complete the material. Urban teachers cannot teach what they don't know, and urban students cannot learn what the teacher cannot teach.

Urban school leaders and teachers don't have to be Christians to understand the immoral and unethical depths of failing to teach urban school students how to read, write, comprehend, and to think. One would assume that thinking is a natural process that occurs effortless. But believe it or not, I never was taught to think as an urban school student. It was only until I entered my first year of college that I was introduced to thinking. Thinking was a new concept to me, but many of my college cohorts seem to be able to think critically just fine. I wondered how was this possible. I had no clue that my school was selling me short. Imagine the anger and betrayal I must have felt. I was a crippled black young man in a system that wasn't ready to hold my hand, but I needed holding. Urban school students must be taught to read, comprehend, and think.

Urban teachers must help lessen the gut-wrenching pain and suffering urban students that experience because of an inadequate education. "Malcom X was palpably angry at the horrible conditions of black life and worked to translate his rage into the redemption of black communities."[83] Martin Luther king also poured his prophetic rage into issues that concerned poverty and racial inequality.[84] Barack Obama worked as a community organizer in the ghettos of Chicago to help eradicate homelessness, hopelessness, crime and poverty.[85] This same tenacity that these individuals have taken to fight for just causes is the same approach teachers and administrators must also take. Urban school students are experiencing tyranny at the oppressive hands of urban schools. Urban school students may not be experiencing direct oppressive measures that stifles their actual liberty, but the inadequacies of urban education are oppressing student's opportunities to succeed. In order for teachers to activate this type of passion about student's ability to learn, they must become enraged about urban schools' unfair educational conditions.

There has always been an expanding, robust debate why urban schools continue to fell urban school students. The discussion hasn't missed the rhetoric needed to hash out solutions. This has never been a problem, I submit. Right now, urban schools are not working for our urban school students. Democracy is weakened and these student's ability to receive a quality education is being denied; moreover, this nation is being denied an educated workforce, instead of given slaves to incarceration, poverty, and homelessness. But this problem mirrors our culture and it will take a cultural shift to change the trajectory of urban school's problems.[86] "We've gone soft as a nation. We have to find a way to reclaim our American competitive spirit. This pertains to many aspects of society, but particularly to the way we're raising our children and the culture that exists in our schools.[87]

This nation's value system has shifted, or maybe they have always been misplaced. We talk about being the biggest, competitive nation in the world, but are we serious. We value athletes more than teachers. We pay them stupid money to hit, shoot, catch or run a ball. Rappers and singers are giving lucrative contracts for their less than prophetic, but damaging rhymes. Society has lost itself alone the way while accruing wealth, power, and prestige. We pay teachers ridiculous meager salaries but expect students to strive to become a teacher someday. What is right about how we reward success? I understand capitalism as well as the next person. How did we decide as a nation that we would devalue teachers, but value entertainers? There is something grossly wrong with this picture. If I'm an urban student, and I have experienced and witnessed poverty my entire life, but when I turn on the television, I see rappers and reality tv show actors living a lifestyle I can only dream, what incentive do I have to pursue academic excellence.

"Black sports often acquired a heroic dimension, as viewed in the careers of figures such as Joe Louis, Jackie Robinson, Althea Gibson, Wilma Rudolph, Muhammad Ali, and Arthur Ashe. Black sports heroes transcended the narrow boundaries of athletics and gained importance as icons of cultural excellence they embodied possibilities of success that were denied to other people of color. But they also captured the obsession with sport as a mean to express black style and as a way to pursue social and economic opportunity."[88]

There is no denying the truth so elegantly and forcefully spoken by Dyson. But society has always given a level of legitimacy to entertainers or athletes. This isn't new to us. I have no reason to demagogue black actors or entertainers. They are like every other American—they just want a piece of the pie. We can't hold them accountable or preach democratic gossip about what society has permitted to happen. It's their job to exploit the opportunities of capitalism. What bothers me is the hypocrisy of this nation's leaders about the failures of public education systems. We can't merely isolate the blame to a specific entity. We are fighting racial, educational and cultural demons that have raped this country of its democratic integrity.

Chapter 14
Black Churches on Every Corner

"Throughout its history, black preaching has been widely viewed as a form of public address brimming with passion but lacking intellectual substance. Like black religion in general, black preaching is often seen as the cathartic expression of pent-up emotion, a verbal outpouring that supposedly compensates for low self-esteem or oppressed racial status. Not only are such stereotypes developed in ignorance of the variety of black preaching styles, but they don't take into account the black churches that boast a long history of educated clergy."[89]

Dr. Dyson is exactly right. There are a variety of preaching styles among the black church. Each preacher attempts to espouse his own style and to execute his own poetic, religious flare while amplifying the Christian, social, and political gospel. To say that all preachers are alike or to assume that the black church clergy speaks without intellectual substance would be a serious and inadequate mischaracterization of the institution.

Historically, the black church has always been the place where African Americans can release their pain and anguish. The black church has always been and will remain just as important as government. In fact, for many blacks, their church is the government. This is hyperbole, but to a degree. For some, the church may serve as a symbolic representative of government. For others, they believe that the church takes the place of the government. In their eyes, government is overrated. The church understands their issues and has a front row seat into their problems. Without the black church in many of these urban communities, they would experience black plight caused by the injustices of social, political, institutional, and economic unfairness. The black church represents a sort of peace and calmness that can't be explained. To walk in one while the spirit is intense, swirling and bouncing off the walls and pews is to understand the emotional and dramatic mental religious shift that takes control of the service. Music playing, drums beating, the first lady singing, the pastor words moving in sync with the drums as he perfectly admonishes the neatly dressed crowd to release and let God have complete control, so that God may do a perfect work in the room.

Dyson puts it this way:

"Our faith can give us the comfort that God walks with us and will not forsake us. That may seem like small solace in the face of our finitude. But the knowledge that God refuses to let us go ultimately calms the soul in distress. That is the only guarantee we have that the universe that has betrayed us at one turn through the perils of nature will stand behind us through the divine Word."[91]

The black church is a pillar in the black community. Often, the leaders can do no wrong in the eyes of its members. The man sometimes is viewed as God, instead of a divine leader. He has unyielding, powerful persuasion. With his eloquent, sophisticated speech and profound religious ideology—he can profoundly suggest or symbolically coerce his members to make life changing decisions. He is seen as King Joffy and ruler and can do no wrong. Many of these Christian churches have taken on cult qualities. Many of their members have excessive and intense admiration for their leader. The man himself can do no wrong—even if he can, he gets a pass. The church becomes their lifestyle. They read, pray, fast constantly. They sacrifice money they don't have. He tells them that they will be blessed thirty, sixty, and ninety-fold for their obedience, and God recognizes their sacrifice. He always needs something. There's a building fund, homeless fund, education fund and the list can become expansive. The giving never stops but the pain and suffering often remains. If this sounds like a rant, it isn't, it's some reflections of my experience. Every black church is guilty of this persona to some degree.

Pursuit for social and economic freedom is masked by seeking religious comfort. They bury their lives in Christian comfort to avoid the pain of the real world. They forsake many of their obligations and responsibilities to the greater community. They forget their civic duties. They use all their talents and gifts only in the church because he tells them. They attend church hoping for a miracle. They believe in divine intervention because he has conditioned their minds and heart to believe. They profoundly believe that God won't allow them to suffer in the face of turmoil or hardship. I have witnessed these events first-hand by personal friends and family members. I am a fervent believer in Christ and his power, but I also am a realist. I see things for what they are and believe that you get out of life what you put in. I see Him as an encourager and disciplinary. I believe he gives you unfounded strength when you most need it. I try not to adopt fairytale principles about how God works. But this is only my ideology. I will return to why I believe this ideological approach is best later.

The central question this chapter begs to be asked and answered is whether the black church has isolated or excluded itself from tackling some of the most social pressing issues of our time. Has it abandoned its obvious responsibility in lieu of selfish pursuit of personal gain that may not always center around religious principles and beliefs? Are churches doing enough to hold black parent's feet to the fire when it comes to teaching their kids to value the education process? Is the church more concern with preaching the religious gospel about social, political and economic injustices that cause great calamity in African American life?

For too many blacks, for too long, the church has been used as a scapegoat. The black church has been used as an excuse to settle, rather educate and sacrifice for the right reasons. It has been used to escape reality, instead of fighting for the change desired or needed. But it's not the church members that deserve the blame. The blame squarely belongs to the church clergy. He preaches the orthodoxy that has forced her into a world of cowardice. His preaching and teaching compel her to seek solace, rather shake up the status quo. She persists in prayer, rather putting her feet to the iron challenging the social ills of society. The black church member leads by example, but his example is well-intentioned, but misplaced. As a result, her offspring sees the passive prayer life she lives, instead of going against the grain to fight for what is right. The off-spring I refer to is the urban student. As a result, the church develops and nurtures a passive parent and the church itself fails to mentor the urban school student community.

Both the church and parent live in a bubble where they both postulate that prayer alone will solve the problem, instead of taking a proactive role to build academic character among urban students. The grand idea to shake up the demons that reside in society is prayer. The mystical force of prayer will solve all the world's challenges. The world can only save itself, if it finds Jesus. This solution alone will solve all the world's problems. This is the belief by many black churchgoers. Because this is their core belief on societal problems, urban students are subjected to urban school policies, instead of the black church and black parent challenging what they know to be inherently wrong. But they are paralyzed by the great "Hope" of prayer. If you remember earlier, I mentioned that I take a more practical approach to religion and faith, so don't be clouded by my stern rhetoric on black churches and faith.

Martin Luther King described it this way when he delivered a sermon in front of members of Calvary Baptist Church. "We say that Jesus has been the most influential character in Western Civilization, and as we read his sermon on the mount there is something about it that penetrates our very souls, but we must remember that at a very early age he sacrificed his time to God, and finally he sacrificed even his life. There are people who expect the best in life without effort. But I tell you ... whatever your potentialities may be, they will amount to little or nothing unless you subject yourself to hard work and discipline."[90]

The urban student is the center of the universe. When we are gone, she remains. What type of world are we leaving behind so she may survive? What type of signal is the church sending by taking a passive, resistant approach to addressing this very important issue? The urban student silently cries to be saved. But the church denies this universal truth because it has convinced itself that everything will be fine. It has convinced itself that God will part the Red Sea as he had once done. It has convinced itself that God will free his people as He had done for the people of Israel by Pharaoh. Because of this fact, many black churchgoers seek refuge from the dark truth. This dark truth I speak of is the tremendous debacle that hunts urban schools that sacrifices urban students subconscious hope and dreams that transcends their understanding.

Black churches and black parents have a duty to serve. The bible notes, "we are God's workmanship, created in Christ Jesus to do good works."[91] In black communities there is an abundance of churches. Heck, it seems like a new church is erected every six months. Think about this fact just for a moment. Think about the true purpose of the institution. Yes, it is designed for people to find solace in times of uncertainty. Yes, it is designed to give preachers a platform to speak truth to power about social and economic issues that plague its community. So, the question remains, if there isn't a shortage of churches, why aren't churches stepping up to help solve this public policy crisis in urban schools. Why aren't they speaking truth to this power to the parents that have students in urban schools? Why aren't they building and fostering relationships with the school community to help solve this problem. They must do more than find reasons to fill their collection plate three times on one Sunday. They must do more than assure its members that prayer alone will protect their children from failing urban schools. They must do more than give their members hope that a bright light shines on the other side of the mountain. Hope and prayer isn't enough. Hope and prayer are the tools that are used after an action plan is set and action is executed.

What hurts is this? The black church understands better than any institution that God's will is perfect, and He "does not give your abilities, interests, talents, gifts, personality, and life experiences unless he intends to use them for his glory."[92] Many urban students will never tap into their gifts. These gifts they possess will remain unlocked potential. The greatest tragedy is to die without realizing your purpose. The black church should want urban students to die empty. That simply means, a person dies after exhausting his purpose and lives out his fundamental reason for existing on earth. Urban students will never reach their highest truest expression.

As adults, we often make the bold assumption and assertion that young people couldn't possibly face real problems. We shake off the notion that they could possibly have the type of problems as an adult. What a flawed, fatal calculation. The faith leaders in black churches have a responsibility to inquire about urban student's welfare. They have a responsibility to take every concern by these students seriously. I think we have convinced ourselves that young people's problems are grossly incomparable to adults. Because we take this approach, the black church focuses too much on helping adults see their way through hardship and place too much emphasis helping adults navigate the lost sea of purpose.

Too many black parents and church leaders are too lazy when it comes to urban student's future. They take a back seat to a problem that demands an aggressive, front seat approach. It is no secret that many black mothers in urban communities are single. They were multiple hats while they battle their own active demons and real issues. I know for my mother, once she found Christ, she took on a persona that only resembled living strictly by the bible and attending as much church as possible. My personal welfare took a back seat to her religion and faith. I won't overgeneralize or paint a broad-brush over faith, religion, and mothers—but it's something to truly consider. The black church must give conscious consideration to helping urban students understand why they exist. Rick Warren puts it this way. "When you attempt to serve God in ways you're not shaped to serve, it feels like forcing a square peg into a round hole. It's frustrating and produces limited results. It also wastes your time, your talent, and your energy. The best use of your life is to serve God out of your shape. To do this you must discover your shape, learn to accept and then develop it to its fullest potential."[93]

Black churches fail at improving urban communities as they profess this is their true calling because they fail to infiltrate and penetrate the hearts and minds of urban students and urban schools. As a result, they fail to achieve what is critically important. They fail to help students visualize, realize and believe how important their existence is. But not merely to exist without evolving, but to transform to a position of conscious understanding to take their righteous places in society. This is a huge responsibility the church is not fulfilling, thus takes for granted. The black church has a duty to teach urban students about their unalienable rights. It must teach urban students not only is it okay to be different, but why it is essential to the greater good of mankind. The black church teaches that God made us uniquely different and those differences are unique to step into our designed purpose. This message can't just be for the elders and adults of the black church. This message must be conveyed to the urban student. I am under a strong impression that urban students need to understand the significance of their existence, and it is more to it than being bamboozled by the miscues of black culture depicted in the media.

The black church needs an overhaul. It needs to teach a new gospel. The good news should reflect a new solidarity that challenges black parents to take up the mantle of parenthood. The black church must emphasize boldness and courage to challenge their urban students and urban schools. Black churches must demand that a new perspective is garnered on this issue. The black church must teach the Christian gospel alone with the education gospel. The gospel is translated to mean "good news." It is good news to realize an urban student has embraced academic rigor. It is good news to know that the black parent takes the journey to support her urban student. It is good news to learn that black parents are holding urban schools accountable for their failed policies. It is good news to learn that urban schools realize the disastrous policies they continue to implement? And, it is good news to learn that the black church fervently preaches and teaches the education gospel as not just something to achieve so that its collection plate "runneth" over, but because the church has brought into this idea that urban students deserve the opportunity to realize their talents, gifts, and intellectual capacities that are necessary to serve and save mankind.

As I understand it, the black preacher fails to let his guard down. He fails to indicate his vulnerability. He takes a "God" like position that depicts more than humanistic qualities. Instead of being relatable by revealing his deepest concerns and problems, he projects a super-natural disposition that deflects what the natural man endures.

Keighton puts it this way. "The preacher has inevitable moments of despair, frustration, and defeat. It cannot be otherwise. He does not live a secluded existence, nor does he merely accept life; he challenges it and seeks to make it nobler, and these very ambitions lead him over difficult path."[94]

The black church spends so much time preaching righteousness and force-feeding religious principles down its members throat, it secludes itself from the world's problems. It isolates itself from some very important issues. The black church cannot hide behind its own bully pulpit—if it desires to effect change. The term church should be synonymous to community. But to achieve this goal, the black church must repair its own image. Black churches cannot be characterized as self-righteousness, morally deceitful, and financially thirsty. The black church tendency to harshly scrutinize and criticize impedes the community from being receptive to its help—that's if it desires to help at all. The black church must establish a blueprint to serve urban students. It must teach them the importance of having a blueprint that guides their very existence.

Martin Luther King eloquently writes this. "I want to ask you a question, and that is, what is in your life's blueprint? This is the most importance and crucial period of your lives, for what you do now and what you decide now, at this age, may well determine which way your life shall go ... now each of you is in the process of building the structure of your lives, and the question is whether you have a proper, a solid, and a sound blueprint ... A life's blueprint should include a deep belief in your own dignity, your own worth, and your own somebodiness. Don't allow anybody to make you feel that you are nobody. The determination to achieve excellence in your various fields or endeavor. You're going to be deciding as the days and the years unfold what ... your life's work will be.... Study hard ... burn the midnight oil... Don't allow anybody to pull you so low as to make you hate them. Don't allow anybody to cause you to lose your self-respect to the point that you do not struggle for justice. However young you are, you have a responsibility to seek to make your nation a better nation in which to live.[95]

King wanted the youth to be convicted about something greater than themselves. He recognized the importance of the youth being able to bring this nation to a point of moral truths. He recognized the power of the youth being able to help transcend social forces that questioned the legitimacy of the black culture. The black church now must help the urban student realize his own necessary conviction. That conviction is—that urban schools subsists in education policies that do not teach the whole student and mislead the urban student about his important role outside of the classroom. The black church must emphatically stress what is at stake. That is, these schools are rolling tide waters of inadequate social progress that threaten black capitalism. Social progress is achieved through democratic ideals of free-speech and protest. The black clergy must frame the issues of race and urban education in such a way that not only is it a sense of fairness and justice to combat equality generated, but also people are made aware that this country would be better off if these problems are seriously addressed and eradicated.

If the black church and its black clergy are serious about addressing black plight, pain, and suffering, it must not ignore failed urban school policies that continue to threaten black democracy. Black freedom is not a universal truth. If the urban student is to truly be free, he must understand the consequences of his own actions. But he must be able to make prudent decisions that will help drive his understanding of this consequential freedom. The black church must begin to educate the urban student about the social ails that exist—seeking to eradicate his freedom. Because we are not a post-racial society—plenty of work needs to be done, but that work won't be completed by the current generation. The next generation must take up this very important work, but he must be properly armed.

Chapter 15
Court Action Part II

As an introduction, this chapter is an imagined response by the current and former Justices on the Supreme Court. I like to take this moment to pay homage to the late great Justice Scalia. One of the original originalists that focused on interpreting the constitution as he believed the founding fathers would have. That said, it has struck me as important to create a surmised dialogue of possible political and philosophical arguments and responses to my present arguments in Court Action part one.

Justice Breyer Response (actual words in quotes): "I have called on lawyers to advocate for better public education, and to give future U.S. citizens the information and tools they need to create a just future for themselves. In July 2007, this court effectively buried *Brown v. Board* by outlawing even voluntary schemes to create racial balance, as practiced by Seattle and Louisville. Furthermore, I must say that inequality in this nation's schools is similar to the institutions of slavery and 50 years of legalized subordination."[96]

By no stretch of the imagination, you have presented very

credible and profound arguments that have rocked the conscious of this Court I believe. There is a general consensus that this country has failed our most vulnerable students. Today, you have articulated very strong and valid arguments why you believe this Court needs to step in. I believe there is a consensus that these students are being let down by every stretch of the imagination. But I must wonder if this is the proper venue to help solve this issue. I have struggled immensely with this question.

But let me assure you that this internal contention has not persuaded or dissuaded me from realizing the seriousness of this problem. Education is the bedrock of democracy as you have so eloquently suggested. Many decades ago, there was a time when being educated was not required. But because we require each child to attend someone's public or private school, this certainly highlights the value our culture places now on education. But that said, I ponder are we really doing these students a just service by insisting they enter into any education system. Unless I am mistaken, I think the idea behind this requirement is to ensure our students get an adequate education.

This Court has set many precedents. Often, it has done so because it has heard the people's resounding, unyielding voices for change. This Court legalized same-sex marriage most recently. Yes, there was strong opposition to this idea, and illuminating dissensions against it. Just because dissents will be expressed, it does not mean that a legal issue lacks merit. Those fighting for some form of justice must hold on to this revelation. I am certain that my friends that hold different beliefs and principles on urban public education will express its doubts about this

Court Action Part II

Court interfering with role of the parent, local communities, and of course, the schools they attend. They are right. Each of them plays significant roles, but I wonder how much each can, and is willing to contribute without legal pressure and persuasion.

It is my genuine concern that we get this issue right as a nation. It is our duty to not sit by as bystanders with no legal, or better yet, moral duty to embrace this issue. We talk about constitutional crisis's often. I believe that these students deserve the right to live out their constitutional guarantees as articulated by this great nation and our founding fathers.

That said, I believe this court has a moral obligation to require local school districts to put in place mandates that will require school leaders and personnel to be held accountable. However, the issue is this, I sit here as only one Justice with limited understanding how to address or resolve this problem. As to mandates, I have no clue as to what they should look like. I remember when this very court mandated that "separate but equal" be no more. The mandate was simple but getting the races to find common ground to integrate was a different and arduous battle. I am under the same impression that this matter poses the same problem. Yes, something needs to be done to ensure these students are being adequately educated, but how does this court help to resolve this problem.

In Thomas Paine's pamphlet entitled "Common Sense," he writes, government exists to secure the freedom and security of its equal citizens and that any government that fails to do so is not worthy of the name, regardless of its pedigree."[97] The phrase "equal citizens" immediately stands out. We must ask ourselves many questions, but the immediate pressing question is, "do we see them as equal citizens." If the answer is yes—they deserve education reform. If the answer is no—education reform will die with this Court. I choose the former. I believe they deserve the type of education reform that requires a shift and focus on holistic education. The petitioner was right to suggest that this Court should seek to be on the right side of history. I do not take this job lightly because my education has afforded me this spectacular opportunity. As a kid, I never imagined sitting on this Court among great minds and forward thinkers. This idea is not lost among me. Urban students deserve the same opportunities as I, so it is my fierce hope and desire that this body sides with my position. The details will have to be figured out on state and local levels, so I hope this body agrees.

Justice Thomas Response (actual words in quotes): *In Parents Involved in Community Schools*, Thomas writes the concurrence. He writes, "today's Court holds that state entities may not experiment with race-based means to achieve ends they deem socially desirable. I wholly concur. Contrary to the dissent's argument, re-segregation is not occurring in Seattle or Louisville; these school boards have no present interest in remedying past segregation; and these race-based student assignment programs do not serve a compelling state interest. Accordingly, the plans are unconstitutional. The dissent would give school boards a free hand to make decisions based on race— an approach reminiscent of that advocated by the segregationists in *Brown v. Board of Education*. This approach is just wrong today as it was a half-century ago. The Constitution and our cases require us to be much more demanding before permitting local school boards to make decisions based on race."

The opponents to my position will express their disdain or even disgust with my arguments, as well as with my constitutional principles. It is no secret that I most certainly strive to adhere to interpreting the constitution the way our founding fathers would have it. Although the Petitioner before this Court is well-intentioned, a fact I cannot deny. But well-intentions are not enough with in this Court. This Court has a serious job, and it cannot be won over by an impassioned plea, or sobering rhetoric that may very well reign true. This is an unfortunate fact that students who attend certain urban schools, may very well be short-changed. But this Court has no place or authority to change the academic paradigm these schools. This takes political will. This is a community fight that needs to be attacked by parents, students, and local leaders. Is it not true that they themselves have the most to lose or gain?

It is not lost on me that I am an African American that sits and holds one of the most distinguished seats of this great nation. No matter how true this fact may be, desegregating schools over a half-century ago was wrong then, as it would be wrong for this Court to even suggest that Petitioner has shown a compelling state interest that mandates this Court has the proper legitimacy to dictate urban school education policies legitimacy. My conscience could never permit me to draw such a conclusion today, nor tomorrow.

I am keenly aware that society is constantly evolving for a plethora of reasons. Because society persists to evolve, such laws must evolve, and new ones written and passed into law. But I cannot say such a measure can be taken by this Court. The laws governing these schools are made on the local level, as they should. This Court has gotten it wrong many times in my opinion. This Court has insisted that liberty and freedom grant the right to trample over the Constitution that our Founding Fathers wrote. In the case of same-sex marriage, I disagreed with the majority. In that instance, I believed that the decision inverted the relationship between a person and the government because human dignity does not succeed from the government. I have long believed that true liberty does not stem from government, but true liberty is to be free from government.

That said, local school districts that comprise of local school boards are charged with this responsibility. This Court would de-legitimatize its very core, if it ruled in favor of Petitioner and his well-intentioned, but feeble legal arguments. The constitution is clear, although many may try to find many ambiguities in it. The Fourteenth Amendment cannot help petitioner on the basis of the legal grounds that he has presented.

Justice Ginsburg Response (actual words in quotes): "The notion that men and women stand as equals before the law was not the original understanding, nor was it the understanding of the Congress that framed the Civil War amendments. Mid-nineteenth-century feminists, many of them diligent workers in the cause of abolition, looked to Congress after the Civil War for an express guarantee of equal rights for men and women. But the text of the Fourteenth Amendment appalled the proponents of a sex equality guarantee. Their concern centered on the abortive second section of the amendment, which placed in the Constitution for the first time the word male. Threefold use of the word male, always in conjunction with the term citizen, caused concern that the grand phrases of the first section of the Fourteenth Amendment—due process and equal protection of the laws—would have, at best, qualified application to women. After close to a century's effort, the suffrage amendment was ratified, giving females the right to vote."

This idea of equality in all public schools is a serious issue. But equality is often highly political. Equality sometimes does not carry out its true meaning or desired intention. Speaking of equality suggest that some policy action must be taken. A policy action that provides a good or service. In this instance, the service is an adequate education. I desperately want to find a way to support this issue, but how do I. Although I ponder in reservation of trying to do what is right and just—do not mistake my sentiment. This perhaps is one of the most important issues of our time. Some of us on this Court recognize the important impact of *Brown* and some of us agree that *Brown* didn't go far enough.

In *Obergefell*, Petitioner argued that the traditional definition of marriage was between a man and woman because it has existed for years. In that instance, hot agitation boiled inside because I was reminded of how feminist like myself had to fight for equality. I was reminded that this was once a testosterone male driven society. But we got beyond that phase because women recognized their self-worth and value and had the gumption to fight for the same types of equality men enjoyed.

I reminded Petitioner that marriage today is not what it was under common law tradition, and under the civil law tradition. Marriage was a relationship of a dominant male to subordinate female. That ended as a result of this court's decision in 1982 when Louisiana's Head and Master Rule was struck down. And no state was allowed to have such a marriage anymore.

The current Petitioner today seeks that same equality. I can't help but to share his views, respect his passion and commitment, but I also must respect this institution. This is far from an easy decision. One hundred percent, Petitioner has backed me into a tight corner, but that corner isn't tight enough. Public education should be a fundamental right. It may be true that urban schools are assaulting the 14th amendment as Petitioner has suggested, but without it being a fundamental right like same-sex marriage, voting, and the freedom to marry the opposite race, I find it difficult to violate constitutional norms. It is not my job to rewrite or misinterpret the constitution. This would be a dangerous voyage to spiral down. This Court has limits and must be bound by such.

At its core, education is a true local issue that requires local stakeholders from all walks of life, and political aisles to address. My most basic principles have taught me that an adequate education opens doors to opportunities unimaginable. No one could have ever told me directly or suggested that I would be sitting in one of the highest, esteemed seats in this great nation of ours. This is a sentiment that we each share on this Court. Only through a proper education, hard work, and determination am I able to be one of nine Justices.

Do I believe these schools are sometimes poorly run and managed? Sure, but that fact does not abolish the fact that this issue is broader and more complex than this Court's understanding. *Brown* marked a tremendous and necessary shift in our social and political culture. I think the arguments posed by the Petitioner are very much credible and share significant resemblance to *Brown*. But *Brown* dealt with segregation and was hoping to heal social and racial wounds among blacks. These were clear violations to the Fourteenth Amendment.

In this case, can you argue based on equal protection grounds that students are being educated differently based on their school districts. I find it hard to believe based on Petitioner's arguments. There are too many factors that play a part in schools and student academic achievement. If Petitioner could make a plausible argument that shows minorities being poorly educated based on their race as opposed to whites, now this would be a case for this Court.

I share petitioner's sentiment for greater accountability and for a more robust adequate education for many of these students. Although, my deeply rooted and humanistic, emotional values would like to persuade myself to hold in favor of Petitioner, the constitution forbids it. This nation has a moral and ethical obligation to educate all students equally, but equal as we have seen, is contextually based. I commend Petitioner for his strength, courage, and resilient spirit to such an admirable cause, but this is the improper venue to change these conditions.

Justice Kennedy Response (actual words in quotes): "The Nation's schools strive to teach that our strength comes from people of different races; creeds, and culture uniting in commitment to the freedom of all. In *Parents Involved in Community Schools* (Parents), these two school districts in different parts of the country seek to teach that principle by having classrooms that reflect the racial makeup of the surrounding community. However, to make race matter now so that it may not matter later may entrench the very prejudices we seek to overcome. In my view, the state mandated racial classifications at issue ... are unconstitutional. ..."

I mention this case to force-feed and embed in your minds that education and its adequacies or inadequacies should not and must not ever be about race and class. Petitioner has not sought to make this a race issue, but he has purposefully, heavily relied on *Brown*. Everything about *Brown* directly suggests and is explicitly about race and equality for blacks. There is no denying that *Brown* forged a new way of seeing race relations, and the way we should think about it, thus engage it. Yes, race is a central part of our universe and undeniably—when we see someone of a different color, prejudices may inadvertently come to mind. So, when I speak of race, it is not to say I don't recognize that it is an ongoing issue in this country. My point is to stress the need to not to see race and how I believe we can get to that point. Is it some idealism on my part, possible, but more optimism as I have described?

The arguments put forth by petitioner in favor of plaintiff's rest wholly on this idea that 14th amendment violations are present. The argument has been pressed that students in urban public schools are being deprived of the opportunity to acquire life, liberty, property and the pursuit of happiness. This argument is loosely made and based on facts that surround failing urban schools. Although, it cannot be denied that many of these schools often times inadequately prepare many urban students—there also are plenty success stories within these schools that adequately prepare students. Sympathy and empathy are not enough alone to change laws in this country. Most recently, I ruled in favor of same-sex marriage. Looking at the issue in retrospect, it embodied more than a privacy right from government interfering with your bedroom or a right to marry whoever you choose. These things certainly are important, but it was more so about the 14th amendment and the principles we value in this country.

I wrote in part. Marriage is sacred to those who live by their religion and offers unique fulfillment to those who find meaning in the secular realm. Its dynamic allows two people to find a life that could not be found alone, for a marriage becomes greater than just the two persons. Rising from the most basic human needs, marriage is essential to our most profound hopes and aspirations. As all parties agree, many same-sex couples provide loving and nurturing homes to their children, whether biological or adopted.... Excluding same-sex couples from marriage thus conflicts with a central premise of the right to marry. Without the recognition, stability, and predictability marriage offers, their children suffer the stigma of knowing their families are somehow lesser. They also suffer the significant material costs of being raised byunmarried parents relegated through no fault of their own to a more difficult and uncertain family life. The marriage laws here thus harm and humiliate the children of same-sex couples.[98] This idea of individual liberty and free will is the true instrument to achieving success. It is the most common way to achieve those things listed within the 14th amendment. In this country we have made the mistake to think that everyone sees or perceives religion the same way. This is one of our greatest blunders as humans. This fact sometimes causes each other to fail because we have trouble accepting each other's views. We can be intolerable as a country. But it's time to explore and exercise tolerance and even acceptance. Disagreements do not make us different. We have more in common than we think—but we must put our narcistic ways aside and promote a spirit of selfless-service. This country is better when it serves. The men and women of law enforcement and arm forces embodies this concept perfectly. By voting in favor of same-sex marriage, it wasn't just about my principles, beliefs, or what I value. We have this unyielding belief that our values are only right. In the same-sex debacle, an important narrative got lost. Children were a part of the equation through no fault of their own.

Urban students are not too blame for their sometimes misfortunes. They don't ask to be born into urban communities no more than we can choose our parents, our race, our wealth, our gifts, or talents. It is settled unwritten law that we cannot control the conditions we are born into, but this country has a responsibility to help students reach for unimagined heights through an adequate education. I fervently believe parents and communities play a vital role to help these students achieve the type of liberty encompassed in the Constitution. But what happens when they fail. Do we just throw in the towel? This is the fundamental question. Petitioner made this point. If we aren't ready to hold parents accountable or punish them for taking a back sit to their kid's education, this nation has a responsibility to do something. We complain about too much of our money goes towards social programs to support the less fortunate, but we fail to do more to fix this crisis at its roots. We can't save every student, but this is about saving more students. We promote individual responsibility but what do you do when you have never been taught responsibility? I think this Court has an overwhelming responsibility to make sure urban schools are committed to urban student success. I agree that a Brown part III is necessary. I also understand the complexity in this statement and the process. I am confident we can work through the details if enough of my colleagues' side with my position.

Justice Sotomayor Response (actual words in quotes): It has been said that it appears that I subscribe to a very liberal judicial philosophy that considers it appropriate for judges to impose their personal views from the bench. This assertion is valid. My judicial philosophy is simple. There is no way the founding fathers could have fathom the type of evolution that this country has faced. An article I read puts it this way. "The constant development of unprecedented problems requires a legal system capable of fluidity and pliancy. Our society would be strait-jacketed were not the courts, with the able assistance of the lawyers, constantly overhauling the law and adapting it to the realities of ever-changing social, industrial and political conditions; although changes cannot be made lightly, yet law must be more or less impermanent, experimental and therefore not nicely calculable. Much of the uncertainty of law is not an unfortunate accident: it is of immense social value." [99]

In *Gant v. Wallingford Board of Education*, "I considered the treatment this lone black child encountered during his brief time in Cook Hill's first grade to have been ... unprecedented and contrary to the school's established policies. ... Only one circumstance in this case stands out as the likely reason for the discrepancy between the defendants' treatment of another struggling students and their treatment of Ray: his race. ... [A] jury could reasonably conclude that the school did not give the black student an equal chance to succeed (or fail)."[100]

Petitioner has stressed a sense of urgency and has rightly compelled this court to rule on the right side of history. I have spent my entire life ruling on the right side of justice because progress is only achieved through those individuals courageous enough to drown out their own selfish motives and personal beliefs. I have spent my entire life fighting for justice and speaking out when injustice is used as a means to cripple someone else's opportunity to succeed in life. I want to believe that this country's' worst and dark days are behind it, but I cannot say this with confidence or assurance. We have a long way to achieve the type of moral justice Martin Luther King consistently described in many of his speeches. But I am not worry about our darkest days because this nation has always found the will and desire to overshadow hate and bigotry. As a country, we must get this issue right. An under-educated, mis-educated or mis-guided people threatens our democracy. Not because they can trample over it or weaken it—but because they are not able to enjoy the type of democracy as I do. This is a sad state of affairs we must come to grips with. Urban students deserve better and I believe this Court has an unyielding responsibility to see that urban schools are properly educating them.

How can this nation sleep restlessly knowing that urban students' academic opportunities are being squandered? Urban students live lives unimaginable and do not have the barest chance to enjoy the silver spoon that your average affluent students enjoy. We live in a nation where capitalism is only achieved by acquiring the best education or maybe working the hardest. If this is the measuring stick, how do we suppose urban students make it beyond their current situations. How do we suppose they strive for something greater, when their exposure has been restricted to their own schools and communities? Petitioner has passionately with force and vigor made these resounding arguments already—but it is worth repeating because I need members of this prestigious body to sincerely think about the grave risk urban students face.

This Court has found the will on many occasions to do what the constitution requires. This Court has recognized that the founders had known way of knowing that this nation would evolve the way it did. I believe the founding fathers firmly and deeply understood this concept. Where we have managed to find common ground has been among the 14th amendment and ordered liberty. This concept of ordered liberty has been prudently used to grant all types of rights. This day cannot and must not be any different. I ask my dear friends on the other side of the political and theoretical aisle not to be dismissive of urban student's less than adequate education. I ask you to put aside your personal jurisprudence and look beyond yourself and your philosophy on big government versus small government. We are not a political body, but we are appointed by presidents that subscribe to our politics and policy preferences. This body is not perfect; neither is the executive and legislative branch. That said, our body is one of supreme importance because we get to solve some of this nation's biggest problems. We get to address issues when the constitution is sometimes silent. We get to address social and political issues that the founders could not fathom during their own time. I believe these ideals are beyond important and necessary to sustain, support, and uphold democracy for all, not a select few in this country.

I think the fundamental question here today is what type of country do we want to be in the future and what type of legacy do you want to leave behind when you are gone? Do you want to be held in high regard as someone that understood that the founders to the Constitution could have not imagined the cultural wars that would exist during your time? Or do you want to be judged as someone who held strict views and philosophical positions that our Constitution does not support. I choose the latter. Of course, this does not come to a surprise, but I ask you to surprise those that subscribe to your politics and political preferences. Political experts, pundits, constitutional and supreme court scholars boast that we are not a political body. Yes, practically speaking, we are not. But in abstract, we are a political body because our holdings subscribe to one side or the other political aisle, which creates our often-divisive politics. There is only one way to drive a wedge between our divisive politics on this issue or to at least make evident to the public that we are align on this issue. We must vote in favor of petitioner. We must collectively sound the alarm that this issue is bigger than Congress or local and state governments. This issue is one that reflects a civil rights crisis for our urban students. Urban students are the unfortunate beneficiaries of urban institution's colossal academic failures. This issue isn't new to us. My morals have long strongly suggested that all persons deserve to participate in true democracy. What better way is this achieved than receiving an adequate education. If these were our kids or grandchildren—we would bend over backwards to solve this issue. I'm asking you to apply the same set of standards—and nothing different. That said, I simply ask this Court to do one thing—that is, the right thing.

Justice Kagan Response (actual words in quote): Throughout American history, the Supreme Court has been a notably conservative institution. The most fruitful years for progressives were Warren's as chief justice. Between 1953 and 1969, Warren was able to radically reshape constitutional law and, with it, America itself. Among the Warren Court's credits ending Jim Crow; establishing one person, one vote; reducing police abuse through new protections for criminal defendant; expanding the freedom of speech; and guaranteeing sexual privacy. Warren didn't accomplish these by embarrassing his colleagues or by making sharper arguments on the merits. Warren was a master politician, one who's sit with the other justices and bring them along slowly and steadily to his side. He sought to understand other justices' concerns and address them. Unlike most of today's justices, Warren was willing to work the halls to gain five votes. Or, in the case of desegregating the schools in *Brown v. Board of Education*, all nine.[101]

During my confirmation process for a seat on the Supreme Court, many senators grilled me about my interpretation on the 1st Amendment because it was widely known that I had not shot a gun before. The senator from Idaho was especially concern because he asked me a series of questions about guns than any other topic. I told this senator, "I'll make a commitment to you that if I'm lucky enough to be confirmed, I will ask Justice Scalia, whom I knew to be a great and active hunter, to take me hunting."[102] As a result, I didn't just go hunting once, I became a regular hunter. I make this point because I strive to always broaden my horizon. I strive to understand those that think differently than me. I have never submitted to being close-minded. I believe that we all can learn from each other. Yes, I have a set of core values that I won't compromise, but individually, we can never know it all. We should never espouse this belief that my principles are best for everyone. This type of thinking will only hurt America and disrupt democracy. It is no secret that I disagree with certain positions that my colleagues endorse on the right. Recently, I was asked how do I approach the Constitution's equal protection and due process clauses.

"While some parts of the Constitution are perfectly clear, the equal protection and due process clauses speak in such abstract, even vague terms. When the Constitution says you're entitled to the due process of law and you're entitled to the equal protection of the law, trying to get that content and meaning—it can't be done by just staring at the words. One approach is to try to figure out what the drafters of the Constitution thought the language meant. I myself, am a big precedent person. I'm kind of what some people call a common-law constitutionalist. I think really hard about how the way of interpreting the due process or equal protection clause has developed over time in case after case and try to think about the principles that have emerged in all those cases."[103]

It is this very important proposition that we must begin with. We must approach due process and equal protection from a position of broad fairness. We must draw our meaning from an evolving standard of decency that mark the progress of a maturing society. One of our fundamental duties in this nation is to protect our youth. Chief Justice William Rehnquist wrote, "the 14th Amendment was intended to protect the people from the state, not to ensure that the state protected them from each other."[104] In the *DeShaney* case, Justice Harry Blackmun dissented with the majority. He wrote, "Poor Joshua!" Victim of repeated attacks by an irresponsible bullying, cowardly, and intemperate father, and abandoned by [welfare officials], who placed him in a dangerous predicament and who knew or learned what was going on, and yet did essentially nothing except recorded the incidents in their files."[105] This is what we are faced with today. We each have the facts. We have long been aware of the tragedies that exist in urban schools and communities. Yet, we sit on the sideline as a non-compassionate body as though we don't have the power to precipitate change.

Urban students deserve the fundamental right not to be abused and neglected by urban school's academic policies. I understand my colleagues on the right seek to strictly construe what the 14th Amendment permits and does not. But this approach demands a broad microscope to compassionately and holistically find in favor of urban students. I respect the rule of law. I respect our system of federalism. This concept of federalism ensures state and local government autonomy, but this does not assure state and local governments that the federal government will relegate to an inferior position when our power is most needed. Our institution is one of the most talked about and sought after to right societies' wrongs. Often, many of those challenges surround our 14th amendment. This is not surprising because we as a nation believe in true liberty. Liberty cannot and shall not recognize race, gender, sex, national origin, or religion. Liberty is liberty and to see it any different is un-American.

In this moment, we have an extraordinary chance to ensure the 14th Amendment works for some of our most deserving young people. I live by the creed that it should not matter where you live in order to receive a fair, just, and adequate education. How much money you have should not determine the quality of education received. Petitioner has made these arguments, and I happen to agree with many of them. As many of my colleagues have suggested, I cannot exactly say what our intervention will look like. But, as petitioner has brought to our attention, when *Brown* was passed the Justices that sat on this Court then were unaware of all the tactics and methods that would be used to change the dynamics of true integration and how those tactics would create tax imbalances that have hurt urban schools. If petitioner is successful, the details will be worked out among important stakeholders that have fought to improve the quality of urban education, state and local government.

Justice Alito Response (actual words in quotes): "Liberty means different things to different people. ... The Court's conception, I said in a [previous] opinion and I believe to be true, is a very postmodern idea; it's the freedom to define your understanding of the meaning of life. Your—it's the right to self-expression. So, if all of this is on the table now, where are the legal limits on it? ... There's no limit. The Court had tried to limit this in some earlier cases from the Rehnquist era, prominently a case called *Glucksberg* that involved the claim that there was a constitutional right that is deeply rooted in the traditions of the country. So, you had to find a strong historical pedigree for this right. ... But the *Obergefell* decision threw that out, did not claim that there was a strong tradition of protecting the right to same-sex marriage, this would have been impossible to find. So, we are at, we are at sea, I think. I don't know what the limits of substantive liberty protection under the 14th Amendment are at this point. ... If it's not in the text of the Constitution or it's not in something that is objectively ascertainable, if it's just whatever I as an appointee of the Supreme Court happens to think is very important, so I don't know where—it raises questions because the more the Court does this sort of thing, the more the process of nomination and confirmation will become like an election. It will become like a political process."[106]

It does not come to any surprise that my colleagues on the other side of the political aisle fervently disagree with my approach to understanding liberty and granting rights based on 14th Amendment protections. But I ask the question, as I have asked many times before, at what point is the Constitution able to live out its true meaning. I happen to think this is important. I happen to think that the Founding Fathers broadly thought about these ideas before we were able to read or understand the Constitution. What gives me cause for concern is the way in which we justify our own beliefs pursuant to the 14th Amendment to create a new right or rights. I didn't particularly agree with the Warren Court but many things that Court did were needed. There is no room for segregation in this country, so the Brown decision was justified. I believe the Founders imagined that day would arise. I imagined they believed that integration would exist, and so the 14th Amendment would be the path to achieving that necessity. But this Court feels entirely warranted in granting such rights like same-sex marriage, for example.

Today, we squarely are faced with an easy decision that this Court has no business or legal authority or merit to supersede state's authority to manage its own public schools. The complexity is overwhelming. *Brown* was necessary and unlike what petitioner is requesting today. And although *Brown* was achieved through a federal mandate, states devised its own plans and methods to execute the federal mandate as petitioner is aware. In fact, petitioner has boldly suggested that *Brown* didn't go far enough, thus this Court has an obligation to right this wrong. I say to petitioner, I respectfully disagree. This Court does not oversee implementations of laws. This Courts mandates a law and expects states to follow through with the law. If states fail to achieve adequate implementation, its citizens may challenge the state's decision or flawed implementation. I repeat, this body does not implement laws. If I were to side with petitioner, States would have to devise and implement a plan to petitioner's request. Frankly, I am clueless as to what petitioner is requesting of this Court. This Court should be spending its time ruling on cases that present legal merit. It is my opinion that petitioner has failed to demonstrate the type of merit required that would justify this Court's time.

Petitioner has chosen to use dark language to describe the problem as he sees it. This tactic will not work with this Court. It may be true that urban students are being deprived or neglected of a fair or adequate education, but there are too many factors that contribute to this problem. For one, too many parents are not good stewards over their kid's education. Parents are and will always be the key to student achievement. Urban schools may be saddled with poor teachers and administrators, but this is not always the case. Parents and students have power. They should let their voices be heard locally. They should air their grievances with the people they take issue with. They should attend school board meetings and mayoral-council meetings to express their concerns. This is their best opportunity to effect change, not here. I applaud petitioner and his supporters, but I ask that you earnestly accept my advice and start there.

Justice Gorsuch Response (Actual words in quote): "It would be a mistake to suggest that originalism turns on the secret intentions of the drafters of the language of the law. The point of originalism, textualism, whatever label you want to put on it—what a good judge always strives to do, and I think we all do—is strive to understand what the words on the page means. Not import words that come from us, but apply what you, the people's representative, the lawmakers, have done. So, when it comes to equal protection of the law, for example, it matters not a whit that some of the drafters of the 14th Amendment were racists, because they were, or sexiest, because they were. The law they drafted promises equal protection of the laws to all persons. That's what they wrote. And the original meaning of those words John Marshall Harlan captured in his dissent in *Plessy*. An equal protection of the laws doesn't mean separate in advancing one particular race or gender—it means "equal." And as I said yesterday, I think that guarantee equal protection of the law's guarantee in the 14th Amendment, that it took a civil war for the constitution, and maybe in all of human history. It's a fantastic thing, and that's why it is chiseled in Vermont marble above the entrance to the Supreme Court of the United States."[107]

As a Justice to the highest court on the land, I have no greater responsibility to mankind. I understand my decisions have life-long and sometimes gut-wrenching ramifications beyond natural understanding. This reason alone prompts me to be a Justice that places grave emphasis on freedom, liberty, and the 14th Amendment that grants access to the sorts of liberty we seek and pursue. As I understand it, the Petitioner precisely makes this argument. He argues that urban students are being deprived of this fundamental concept of ordered liberty. He has passionately articulated why he believes urban schools are intentionally or unintentionally exploiting urban students' and their less than

Court Action Part II

flattering social and economic conditions to support the prison-to-pipeline scheme. I must say these are very strong assertions and arguments that Petitioner makes.

It is no secret that this Court has ruled that students do not lose their rights once they enter school buildings. Students still have a right to express themselves within reason and so long as it does not disrupt the learning process. Students have the right to a safe environment. Students have a right to express their religious views without schools endorsing one religious' organization over another. Students with disabilities have a protected right to be treated fairly, normal, and the right to engage the learning process as students without disabilities are able. Now, we are even face with bathroom access for transgender students. "*In A.M. v. Holmes* (2016), I dissented from a decision by a conservative colleague upholding the arrest and handcuffing of a 7th grader who disrupted a class by repeatedly generating fake burps. I pointed out to several state-court rulings criminalizing conduct only where it substantially interfered with the actual functioning of the school, rather than momentarily diverting attention from classroom activity.[108] All that said, it is important to balance individual rights and school authority.

Today, we are faced with a different problem according to Petitioner's legal brief. We are dealing with the type of rights that are easily identifiable. We are dealing with the idea or concept of an adequate education. It is clear that Petitioner believes that urban school's education policies are outdated, and that urban schools are failing at devising and implementing the type of culture needed to help urban students succeed. We know that an education determines so much of a person's life. An equal, fair, just, and equitable education can change lives. All of our success stories stem from a great education and great teachers. What teachers do every day is beyond incredible. They are the true heroes, and no one can dispute this fact. On the other side of the coin, we also know that an unjust, unfair, inequitable, and inadequate education often renders opposite results. Poor academic schools fail to help urban students to tap into their hidden potential. Poor academic schools give urban students' false hope about their future. Poor academic schools fail to instill the value of hard work, discipline, and dedication to achieve goals. In fact, poor academic schools fail to instill the value of goal setting for urban students. Sadly, these are the facts as we have come to know them. All that said, I still find it hard today to rule in favor of Petitioner.

Yes, there is a need for drastic academic change in urban schools, but that responsibility does not squarely fall on urban schools. Parents, grandparents, clergymen, community leaders, business leaders and non-governmental organizations must take the lead to bring about the type of change Petitioner is advocating. States have regulatory authority over its schools, and the federal government supports those efforts. School districts know no best how to teach its students. And if parents are concerned with its education system, they should air those concerns to local school boards, departments of education and state leaders. This Court has no place in this matter. Essentially, this is a political matter, and not a legal matter. I will re-emphasize that I agree with many of Petitioner's arguments, but this Court just doesn't have the power to mandate what Petitioner has requested. As many of my other colleagues have expressed, *Brown* was different. *Brown* was more than about integrating schools. *Brown* was about healing social and racial vestiges that has plagued this nation far too long. *Brown* was about creating a new democracy in this nation and making certain the 14th Amendment lived up to its promised moral creed. *Brown* was about forging a new path for race relations and reconciling perceived racial differences. That said, I think Petitioner has created important national attention to this issue. I think his efforts will not go in vain. It is my hope that all urban communities rise in unison and take this fight to the local level.

Chief Justice Roberts (actual words in quotes): The question considered by the Court was whether a public school can voluntarily classify students by race and use racial classifications to make school assignments if the school district had never been found to have legally segregated its schools or had been released from a court-ordered desegregation plan. I alone with four other justices ruled that the Seattle and Louisville plans violated the Constitution. Because racial classifications are potentially harmful, Court precedent has subjected plans using racial classifications to "strict scrutiny requires that the government show a compelling interest in achieving the goal for which racial classifications are being used, and also that the plan has been narrowly tailored to achieve that goal. Looking back at its prior rulings, the plurality found that the Court had recognized two compelling government interests in the educational context. The first is a compelling interest in remedying the effects of intentional discrimination. The second was a compelling interest in student body diversity in a higher education setting. "We noted that the Seattle schools were never legally segregated and that a court had found that the metropolitan Louisville schools had eliminated the "vestiges" of past segregation to the extent capable." As a result, "they argued that government action to remedy societal (rather than government) actions that discriminate are not within the realm of constitutional actions."[109]

We find ourselves in quite interesting times. The arguments made by the Petitioner are somewhat interesting. Creative lawyering is important in the legal field, especially to acquire great success. The Petitioner has vigorously and relentlessly pressed the point that urban schools are assaulting the 14th amendment. Thus, he further argues that not only are urban schools committing such acts, these schools are intentional in their actions. Those are strong claims that I believe are based on raw emotions. Petitioner's heart undoubtedly is in the right place, so I do not blame him for his bold assertions. But this Court does not come to conclusions based on emotions. We focus on the constitution and what has been established as precedent as much as possible. I admit, there are times when certain decisions require new ways of looking at an amendment from the constitution. This is are not one of those instances.

It is clear that Petitioner looks to the 14th amendment for success. The 14th amendment has given us much trouble in the past, and I presume it will continue to give us more trouble. To seek freedom is always controversial. It's controversial because it includes the ability to pursue life, liberty and property. It

Court Action Part II

solidifies for an individual that I can now move forward with less obstacles or roadblocks. We have experienced this too often in our nation's history. The abolishment of slavery comes to mind and what was at stake. This was a pivotal period in our history. A movement to desegregate schools and other public institutions. A movement to ensure women could share in equality like men. I'm also reminded of opposite races having the right to marry without being jailed. We have always been an imperfect nation, but what drives our perfection is our ability to learn from our mistakes.

Petitioner's arguments have a sort of *Brown* feeling as he has creatively argued that *Brown* didn't go far enough. Over the years, many urban school supporters have made similar arguments. We are clear that Brown was ultimately about remedying discrimination and to integrate public schools regardless of race. As this was an intense period in our society, many whites fought this law. Many whites established private schools to evade the law. Because of this fact, many believe that Brown truly didn't achieve its goal. Some of that may be true. But Brown did have great success from integration to funding. The hope of integration was to secure more funding for minorities. This was achieved. The funding issue is a problem now because of the up rise of suburban communities. But minorities are representative in suburban communities across the country. There is something in public policy called "vote with your feet." That simply means you move where policies are more favorable to your liking. However, I understand when you are poor you can't just up and move your family to a suburb, so your son or daughter can attend a better school. Here lies the problem and what Petitioner is arguing.

All that said, the argument Petitioner makes is not a problem this Court can begin to fix. This is a true local and state issue. This Court does not have the intellectual capacity to understand the problems urban schools face. Parents, teachers, administrators, community groups and other stake holders must take this fight to school boards and state legislatures. He is challenging the way in which urban schools are operated. He indicates that it's a culture problem in these schools. This sounds like urban schools must do a better job and parents must seek to hold them accountable. Petitioner should take his energy and passion to galvanize more parents to step up and speak out about what they see as inadequate education. I agree with the other justices that this Court does not have the proper jurisdiction to rule in favor of the Petitioner and this matter must be handled locally.

Author's Note

Sitting down to write this book has been a real joy and has also served as therapy. Yes, therapy. For years I desired to write a book about urban schools, but I was afraid and just didn't know what approach to take on such a serious inquiry. When I realized my premise, I became excited and disappointed at the same time. But I won't dwell on what I have countlessly expressed throughout this book already. The true reason for this small letter to you is to explain my motivation and intent behind the book. I want to be super clear why the tone you have experience throughout the book exist.

The words expressed are somber. The words expressed are sometimes harsh or even overtly and overly critical. Yes, I stand by every word written. But I also have hope in urban schools as well. I believe urban schools are embattled with tremendous odds as they seek to educate many students that just do not value or understand the importance of education. So, I get it. Urban teachers and administrators have difficult jobs. What's worse, these teachers are not paid adequately, which would provide them with more incentive to do more than their required jobs. So, again, I get it and have great sympathy for their situations. However, this book needed to be written. Not to insult urban schools, but to shine a light on this public policy crisis. Poor education just doesn't affect urban students, it touches our economy in so many ways.

Also, I thought it was important to share my experiences as an urban student, mentor and ex-educator to help the world realize what really happens in these schools. I also wanted teachers to realize the impact they can have on a student—good or bad. Ultimately, I chose the title because I believe it to be provocative and may incite passionate arguments on both sides. I believe I have achieved that goal beyond my wildest imagination. But you will be the judge.

Finally, I hope you read this book with an open mind, especially if you are an educator or an ex-educator. However, I understand some will be offended. That's unfortunate because I stand by every criticism offered. To that point, although I have leveled some strong criticisms, I believe these schools can be fixed. Yes, it will take total effort by many stakeholders, but urban schools must be more aggressive in action, and less aggressive with its rhetoric.

ACKNOWLEDGMENTS

The reason I exist and persist to seek and achieve my goals is simple. My mother Diane McCullough, a woman of superb faith, has modeled a life of commitment and selfless service to her faith, family, and community. I marvel at the accomplishments that she has achieved even through so much adversity, but she has always been my rock and inspiration. As a side note, she and I both graduated from Tougaloo College together where we earned our first undergraduate degree together. What a moment in time that was. My second rock, my aunt Cathy McCullough. She is the historian of the family and the one everyone seeks for advice unquestionably. When she speaks, you listen, period. I can remember countless times calling her to cry out about why it seemed like the world was against me. She never wavered or not responded. Her words are always timely and on point. I can still hear her speaking to me when my spirit is low, and I constantly seek her opinions and advice to this day.

I would lie if I didn't say that growing up without a father was difficult. Many black men do it. It is the new norm—I get it. But not having one had some devastating effects on my life, but still I rise. I rose when the nay sayers didn't extend their help or didn't believe in me. But luckily, I had four women that were a part of my life.

My aunt Jackie got me through some very difficult times. She has no kids, but it is no doubt that I am the son she never had. I am tearing up just thinking about the support she has given me. She was that go to aunt. She never told me no and now treats my boys the exact same way. I am truly grateful.

Last but not least. My aunt Constance, the pragmatist. She wasn't around as much because she moved away. But she was still key to many of my choices. Whenever I needed to hear words that involved less fluff, she was my go-to person. She tells you how it is and refuses to skirt around what is possible and not possible.

I must give a shot out to my only sister, Michelle and my awesome nephews, Micah (14) and Bryson (10). She is a single parent who works harder than any single parent I have witnessed in my life. But I am thankful to be a father to my nephews. See, the Lord has giving me great responsibility to raise my boys, nephews and mentor other young black boys with absent fathers. I take this job serious and do not take it for granted. All that said, I just want to thank the women in my family for driving me towards success. Our family is filled with educators, doctors, lawyers, businessmen-women, now an author.

I would be remiss if I didn't dedicate this book to my grandmother, who has been ill my entire life. She doesn't know all the great things I am doing, but I can imagine she has a good idea. I love you so much. Finally, I would like to thank Justin, Carlton, Kabah, Kimberly, and Karla. These individuals have acquired tons of success. I watched their lives to pattern mine after. They don't know this, but I did. I am truly in their debt.

I saved the best for last. Thank you, God! He is the source of this book. The setbacks I have endured have been ever constant and unyielding. I believe he had to birth this book out of me, so that I may enter into the next phase of my life. I am unaware of that phase, but I am certain He will reveal it when it is time.

To leave comments regarding my work, send me an email at mlawmccullough@gmail.com or locate me on Facebook to leave a comment.

Thanks

References

(Endnotes)

[1] Ibid.

[2] Ibid.

[3] Ibid.

[4] Martin Luther King, Jr., *A Testament of Hope: The Essential Writings and Speeches*, (New York, New York, HarperSanFranciso, 2003).

[5] Ibid.

[6] Beverly Daniel Tatum, Why Are All The Black Kids Sitting Together In The Cafeteria: *And Other Conversations About Race*, Basic Books, New York, (2017).

[7] https://www.americanprogress.org/issues/education-k-12/news/2017/12/19/444212/new-path-school-integration (December 2017).

[8] Michael J. Klarman, *From Jim Crow to Civil Rights: The Supreme Court and the Struggle for Racial Equality* (2004).

[9] Daria Roithmayr, Reproducing Racism: How Everyday Choices Lock In White Advantage (New York: NYU Press, 2014), Kindle Edition, location 732.

[10] Paul Butler, Black Male Exceptionalism: *The Problems and Potential of Black Male-Focused Interventions,* Georgetown University Law Center (2013).

[11] Lerone Bennett, The Crisis of the Black Male (1983).

[12] Ruth Neild and Robert Balfanz, An Extreme Degree of Difficulty: *The Educational Demographics of Urban Neighborhood High Schools, Journal of Education for Students Placed at Risk*, 11(2), 123-141, Lawrence Erlbaum Associates, Inc. (2006).

[13] https://www.nbcnews.com/business/business-news/back-school-older-students-rise-college-classrooms-n191246.

[14] Monique Morris, Push Out: *The Criminalization of Black Girls in School*, (New York: New York Press, 2016).

[15] Ibid

[16] Angela J. Davis, Katheryn Russell-Brown, Stephen A. Saltzburg, Daniel J. Capra and Michael E. Tigar, Policing the Black Man: *Arrest, Prosecution and Imprisonment,* New York, New York, Pantheon Books (2017).

[17] *Jenifer Gratz and Patrick Hamacher, Petitioner v. Lee Bollinger et. Al.*, 539 U.S. 244 (2003).

[18] *Swann v. Charlotte-Mecklenburg Board of Education,* 402 U.S. 191 S. Ct. 1267; 28 L. Ed. 2d 554; 1971.

[19] Michael J. Klarman, Unfinished Business: *A History of Racial Equality in America* (New York: Oxford University Press, 2007).

[20] Ibid.

[21] Ibid.

[22] Ibid.

[23] Ibid.

[24] Center for Public Education, http://www.data-first.org/data/how-much-money-does-our-school-district-receive-from-

federal-state-and-local-sources/, How much money does our school district receive from federal, state, and local sources?

²⁵ Ibid.

²⁶ http://www.wdam.com/2018/09/06/mississippi-education-funding-causes-concerns (September 6, 2018).

²⁷ Michael Dyson, Can You Hear Me Now: *The Inspirations, Wisdom, and Insight of Michael Eric Dyson,* (New York, New York, Civitas Book, 2009).

²⁸ Beverly Daniel Tatum, Why Are All The Black Kids Sitting Together In The Cafeteria, 2017.

²⁹ Monique Morris, Push Out, 2016.

³⁰ Ibid.

³¹ Ibid.

³² Michelle Rhee, Radical: *Fighting to Put Students First,* (New York, New York, Harper-Collins, 2013).

³³ https://www.mdek12.org/OPR/Reporting/Accountability/2019.

³⁴ Ibid.

³⁵ Ibid.

³⁶ Michael Eric Dyson, The Black Presidency, 2017.

³⁷ Ibid.

³⁸ Monique Morris, *Push Out, 2016.*

³⁹ https://docsouth.unc.edu/neh/douglass/douglass.html.

⁴⁰ Ibid.

⁴¹ Ibid.

[42] https://books.google.com/books?hl=en&lr=&id=e_CxRsMZ-6oC&oi=fnd&pg=PR7&dq=john+dewey+theory&ots=oaUuUQs4Rz&sig=TmcKQJGMq4Zg-xK_bPN6vvkW.

[43] Edmund Burke and Thomas Paine, The Great Debate: *The Birth of Right and Left*, New York, New York, Basic Books (2104).

[44] David Salisbury and Latique Jr., Casey, Educational Freedom in Urban America: *Fifty Years after Brown v. Board of Education*, Washington, D.C., Cato Institute (2004).

[45] Michelle Rhee, Radical: *Fighting to Put Students First,* (New York, New York, Harper-Collins, 2013).

[46] Jan Hughes and Oi-man kwok, "Influence of Student-Teacher and Parent-Teacher Relationships on Lower Achieving Readers' Engagement and Achievement in the Primary Grades," *Journal of Educational Psychology 99*, no. 1 (2007): 39-51.

[47] Kristin Henning, Jenadee Nanini & Geoff Ward, *Toward Equal Recognition, Authority, and Protection: Legal and Extra-legal Advocacy for Black Youth in the Juvenile Justice System,* in RIGHTS, RACE, AND REFORM: 50 YEARS OF CHILD ADVOCACY IN THE JUVENILE JUSTICE SYSTEM 30-50 (Kristin Henning, Laura Cohen & Ellen Marcus eds., New York: Routledge 2018).

[48] Angela Davis, Policing the Black Man, 2017.

[49] Monique W. Morris, Push Out, 2015.

[50] Ibid.

[51] Ibid.

[52] Angela Davis, Policing the black Man, 2017.

⁵³ Angela Caputo, http://www.chicagotribune.com/news/watchdog/ct-dui-checkpoints-chicago-met-20150507-story.html.

⁵⁴ Ibid.

⁵⁵ Angela Davis, Policing the Black Man, 2017.

⁵⁶ https://www.constitutioncenter.org/learn/educational-resources/constitution-faqs, National Constitution Center.

⁵⁷ The Library of Congress, www.americaslibrary.gov/jb_recon_revised_1.html

⁵⁸ Ibid.

⁵⁹ Carlotta Walls Lanier and Lisa Frazier Page, *A Mighty Long Way: My Journey to Justice at Little Rock Central High School*, One World Books Publishing, (2010).

⁶⁰ Ibid.

⁶¹ Ibid.

⁶² Ibid.

⁶³ William Love Boyd, *President Reagan Report on Public Education*, edweek.org (October 2019).

⁶⁴ Michael Eric Dyson, The Black Presidency, 2017.

⁶⁵ Ibid.

⁶⁶ *West Virginia State Board of Education v. Barnette,* 319 U.S. 624.

⁶⁷ *National Association for the Advancement of Color People for Color People v. Alabama,* 357 U.S. 449.

⁶⁸ Monique W. Morris, Push Out, 2015.

⁶⁹ Michelle Rhee, Radical, 2013.

70 Ron Allen and Leah Smith, African American teachers push messages of affirmation, success at Philadelphia school, https://www.nbcnews.com/news/us-news/african-american-teachers-push-messages-affirmation-success-philadelphia-school-n883661 (June 16, 2018).

71 Ibid.

72 Monique W. Morris, Push Out, 2015.

73 Michael Eric Dyson, Can You Hear Me Now: The Inspiration, Wisdom, and the Insight of Michael Eric Dyson, Basic Civitas Books, (2009).

74 Michael Eric Dyson, The Black Presidency, 2017.

75 Ibid.

76 Beverly Daniel Tatum, Why Are All Blacks Sitting Together in the Cafeteria, 2017.

77 Ibid.

78 Martin Luther King, Jr., *A Testament of Hope, 2003*.

79 Michael Eric Dyson, The Black Presidency, 2017.

80 David Salisbury and Latique Jr., Casey, Educational Freedom in Urban America, 2004.

81 Ibid.

82 Ibid.

83 Ibid.

84 Michael Eric Dyson, The Black Presidency, 2017.

85 Ibid.

86 Barack Obama, The Audacity of hope, (The Penguin Random

House, New York, New York, 2007).

[87] Michelle Rhee, Radical, 2013.

[88] Ibid.

[89] Michael Eric Dyson, Can you Hear me Now, 2009.

[90] Ibid.

[91] Patrick Parr, The Seminarian: *Martin Luther King Jr. Comes of Age*, Lawrence Hill Books, (2018).

[92] Rick Warren, The Purpose Driven Life: What on Earth Am I Here For, Zondervan (2012).

[93] Ibid.

[94] Ibid.

[95] Patrick Parr, *The Seminarian*, 2018.

[96] Ibid.

[97] Justice Breyer, quotes.net/author/Supreme+Court+Justice+Stephen+Breyer.

[98] Edmund Burke and Thomas Paine, The Great Debate, 2014.

[99] Andrew Soergel, https://www.usnews.com/news/articles/2015/06/26/9-need-to-know-quotes-from-the-obergefell-v-hodges-opinions, June 26, 2015.

[100] Michael C. Dorf, *What is Sonia Sotomayor's Judicial Philosophy?* https://supreme.findlaw.com/legal-commentary/what-is-sonia-sotomayors-judicial-philosophy.html (June 2009).

[101] Erik W. Robelen, School Rulings by Sotomayor Eyed Carefully, https://www.edweek.org/ew/

articles/2009/06/10/33sotomayor-2.h28.html, Education Week (June 2009).

[102] Adam Winkler, The Coming of the Kagan Court: Why Elena Kagan is the most influential liberal justice, http://www.slate.com/articles/news_and_politics/jurisprudence/2013/10/elena_kagan_is_the_most_influential_liberal_justice.html, (October 6, 2003).

[103] Ibid.

[104] Michael Hotchkiss, Kagan discusses the Constitution, the Supreme Court and her time at Princeton, https://www.princeton.edu/news/2014/11/21/kagan-discusses-constitution-supreme-court-and-her-time-princeton (November 21, 2104).

[105] Jess Bravin, *Kagan Backed Broad Interpretation of 14th Amendment*, https://www.wsj.com/articles/SB10001424052748703745904575248620872377444 (May 16, 2010).

[106] Ibid.

[107] Adam White, Justice Alito: Judicial Restraint Amidst The Court's 'Postmodern' Activism, https://www.weeklystandard.com/adam-j-white/justice-alito-judicial-restraint-amidst-the-courts-postmodern-activism (July 20, 2015).

[108] Paul Crookston, *Gorsuch: A Mistake to Say That Originalism Turns on thee Secret Intent of the Drafters*, https://www.nationalreview.com/corner/neil-gorsuch-explains-originalism-dianne-feinstein-citing-14th-amendment/ (March 22, 2017).

[109] Clint Bolick, Gorsuch, the judicious judge, https://www.educationnext.org/gorsuch-the-judicious-judge-supreme-court-education/ (Summer 2017/Vol. 17, No.3)

[110] Michelle Parrine, Across the Color Line: Diversity, Public Education and the Supreme Court, National Council for the Social Studies, 2008.

www.ingramcontent.com/pod-product-compliance
Lightning Source LLC
Chambersburg PA
CBHW071353290426
44108CB00014B/1535